ON CRUELTY AND THE LAW

By Daniel S. Alcorn

Sterling Letter
PRESS

TABLE OF CONTENTS

I. INTRODUCTION

"Man is the cruelest animal." — Friedrich Nietzsche

The subject of cruelty is difficult to discuss. It brings together a number of seemingly unrelated topics. It conjures up disturbing images and concepts, and it understandably tends to make people uncomfortable. By the same token, and likely due to that tendency, cruelty is a mainstay of popular music, fiction literature, and art (especially film). Some modern music (particularly but not exclusively from the rap genre) is so graphically misogynistic and violent in nature as to potentially be considered cruel.[1] Modern filmmaker Quentin Tarantino has a particular flair for depicting cruelty and violence in his films including *Reservoir Dogs*, *Pulp Fiction*, *Django Unchained* and *The Hateful Eight* to name a few. Additionally, the *Saw* series of horror films from a different filmmaker, with the first being released in 2004, was critically acclaimed and garnered record revenues by depicting a killer who tests his victims' will to live by putting them through deadly "games" where they must inflict great physical pain upon themselves to survive.

Of course, "art imitates life"[2] so naturally there is no shortage of cruelty in real life. In fact, to some extent, participants in our modern life and culture have become desensitized to cruelty as a result of its seeming ubiquity. Despite its distasteful nature, the subject of how the law addresses cruelty, and particularly cruelty to humans, is the focus of this essay. We should not shy away from difficult topics, as it seems that when we become uncomfortable discussing a subject

---

[1] See SNOOP DOGG, *Bitches Ain't* Shit, *on* THE CHRONIC (Death Row Records 1992) ("Bitches ain't shit but hoes and tricks. Lick on these nuts and suck the dick."); JASPER DOLPHIN, *Bitch Suck Dick*, *on* GOBLIN (XL Recordings 2011) ("Once again I gotta punch a bitch in her shit. I'm icy bitch, don't look at my wrist. Because if you do, I might blind you bitch."); EMINEM, *Kill You*, *on* THE MARSHALL MATHERS LP (Aftermath Entertainment and Interscope Records 2000) ("Slut, you think I won't choke no whore. Til the vocal cords don't work in her throat no more?").

[2] Aristotle

we are then actually making some small measure of progress toward understanding and hopefully alleviating it.

Cruelty is part of human nature. We engage in it. It is clear that we are both repulsed by cruelty and at the same time mesmerized and sometimes even entertained by it. We adopt laws in an effort to regulate and curb certain aspects of human nature, including cruelty. "All laws are an attempt to domesticate the natural ferocity of the species."[3] For the most part, the law abhors cruelty. On the other hand, the law has difficulty in defining it and differentiating it from appropriate conduct (i.e, proper forms of punishment). In some instances, cruelty is not only countenanced by the law but actually promoted by the law.

No attempt is made here to inventory the myriad forms and examples of cruelty which have existed and do now exist in Western society. Neither is this essay intended to contain an extensive philosophical or psychological discussion of cruelty or human dignity itself. Nor does this essay concern itself with the mundane, run-of-the-mill, mean things and wrongs we regularly perpetrate on each other. This essay is not about morality. Rather, this essay is intended to illuminate the developments in our law designed to identify and either implement or combat true cruelty, whether state-sponsored or individual in nature.

This essay is inspired by a recent trip to Rome, Italy, which included the almost obligatory tour of the ruins of the ancient Colosseum, an icon of the Roman Empire. Impressively constructed under several Roman Emperors around 80 AD, the Colosseum is an oval amphitheater located near the center of Rome. At its zenith, it held approximately 50,000 to 80,000 spectators who clamored to obtain coveted tickets to be entertained by gladiatorial contests and public

[3] John W. Gardner, S.F. EXAM'R, July 3, 1974.

spectacles including executions, re-enactments of famous battles, and dramas based on Roman mythology.

Most have at least a passing familiarity with the type of inhumane practices sponsored by the Roman government at the Colosseum. Movies like *Ben-Hur* and *Gladiator* speak to the cruelty of the Romans exhibited at the Colosseum. However, nothing compares to a tour narrated by a local guide with a gift for history. Perhaps the best illustration of how torturous it was is that self-castration was regularly offered as an alternative to a painful death in the arena. A slave or criminal was given the alternative to cut off his own testicles in front of the gathered Roman masses and live out his life as a slave and eunuch rather than being publicly killed in some grotesque fashion. These practices lasted until the early medieval era when the structure ceased being used for "entertainment" purposes. It was the history of that place that sparked reengagement with the problem of cruelty. The abject inhumanity displayed by the Romans at the Colosseum causes one to ponder how Western civilization has evolved, and not evolved, over the last two millennia when it comes to cruelty and the law.

II. WHAT IS CRUELTY?

While it is not the mission of this essay to provide an exhaustive examination of the philosophy of cruelty, it does help to have a working understanding of the term to discuss it in the context of the law. The term "cruelty" can be defined in several ways and contexts.

A. Black's Law Dictionary

Black's Law Dictionary defines cruelty as "The intentional and malicious infliction of physical or mental suffering upon a living creature, especially a human."[4]

B. The Encyclopedia of World Problems and Human Potential

The Encyclopedia of World Problems and Human Potential defines "cruelty" as follows:

> Cruelty is the wilful infliction of unnecessary pain and suffering, *i.e.* pain and suffering that are not necessary to achieve morally important ends and thus cannot be justified by those ends. Cruelty is the infliction of pain and suffering for their own sake on any sentient creature that can experience pain and undergo suffering. It can be physical, emotional or spiritual. It can be directed toward humans or other animals and, some would suggest, toward plants. It is destructive toward both the perpetrator and the victim.[5]

C. Merriam-Webster's Dictionary

The Merriam-Webster's Dictionary defines "cruel" as "disposed to inflict pain or suffering: devoid of humane feelings"[6], and "cruelty" as "the quality or state of being cruel".[7]

Synonyms for "cruelty" include: barbarity, brutality, heartlessness, sadism, savagery and viciousness.

D. Professor Paulo Barrozo's Four Conceptions of Cruelty

According to law professor, Paulo Barrozo, there are four distinct conceptions of cruelty in the context of criminal law.[8] "The differences between these conceptions of cruelty rest on the

---

[4] *Cruelty*, BLACK'S LAW DICTIONARY (11th ed. 2019).
[5] Union of International Associations, *Cruelty*, THE ENCYCLOPEDIA of WORLD PROBS. & HUM. POTENTIAL, http://encyclopedia.uia.org/en/problem/149119 (July 7, 2019, 9:52 PM).
[6] *Cruel*, MERRIAM-WEBSTER.COM DICTIONARY, https://www.merriam-webster.com/dictionary/cruel (Jan 24, 2022).
[7] *Cruelty*, MERRIAM-WEBSTER.COM DICTIONARY, https://www.merriam-webster.com/dictionary/cruelty (Jan 25, 2022).
[8] Paulo Barrozo, *Cruelty in Criminal Law: Four Conceptions*, 51, CRIM. L. BULL. no.5, 1025, 1026 (2015).

types of agency, victimization, causality, and values that they employ."[9] In his somewhat abstruse essay, Barrozo examines the philosophy of Michel de Montaigne,[10] Lucius Annaeus Seneca the Younger,[11] and Thomas Aquinas,[12] among others in his work. He also cites numerous United States Supreme Court Eighth Amendment cases.

The first of Barrozo's conceptions of cruelty is the agent-objective conception, which is "exemplified by punitive agency that goes above in degree and beyond in type the punishment allowed by applicable norms."[13] Under this conception, the victim suffered cruelty in light of "the objective character of the act or treatment" she was subjected to. Cruelty, in this sense, is defined as an "inclination of the mind toward the side of harshness." Any punishment or other treatment that surpasses the scope of sufficiency and ventures into possibility is classified as excessive, and therefore, cruel.[14]

The second conception is agent-subjective, in which "cruelty obtains only when the agent's deviant behavior is accompanied by the fault of character consisting in deriving personal delight from causing and witnessing suffering."[15] This conception is best understood under the presumption that punishment or other violence is a means to restore the offset in the cosmic order of the universe caused by wrongdoing. Anything that goes beyond what is necessary for this restoration, then, is cruel; the peace and harmony is not balanced with excessive punishment or

---

[9] *Id.*
[10] Michel de Montaigne is widely regarded as one of the most important 16th Century writers. Montaigne was a French aristocrat. He wrote an essay on cruelty in which he attributes his hatred of cruelty to his natural softness. He addresses the topic from an experiential point of view, appealing to human sensibility and focusing on the element of suffering.
[11] Lucius Annaeus Seneca the Younger (Seneca) was a Roman Stoic philosopher. He wrote extensively on the topic of moral issues, and his works are essential to ancient Stoicism.
[12] Thomas Aquinas was an Italian Dominican friar and Catholic priest. He was also an immensely influential philosopher.
[13] Barrozo, *supra* note 10, at 1035.
[14] *Id.* at 1035-1038.
[15] *Id.* at 1039.

violence—the scale of wrongdoing merely tips to the other side. For example, the Eighth Amendment of the U.S. Constitution prohibits cruel and unusual punishment, which means that we must "inquir[e] into a prison official's state of mind [...]" when determining that the agent is not taking pleasure in inflicting pain and that punishment does not exceed the crime.[16]

The third conception is victim-subjective, in which the "element of cruelty rests in the victim's intense experience of suffering."[17] Here, the pain or the sense of degradation and humiliation experienced particularly and uniquely by the victim is considered. Recognizing cruelty, then, requires reference to our compassion rather than some normative standard of reasonableness. Continuing with the example of punishment, the state's intention is not relevant in determining whether a punishment is cruel. According to the law, "ill-treatment must attain a minimum level of severity," and this minimum is determined by "all the circumstances of the case, such as the duration of the treatment, its physical or mental effects and, in some cases, the sex, age, and state of health of the victim, etc."[18]

The fourth and final conception is the accumulation of all the prior conceptions: the victim-objective and agent-independent. In this conception, Barrozo explains:

> By relying upon the suffering of victims, victim-subjective conceptions fail to capture instances of cruelty in which the victim is deprived of his senses or consciousness about his predicament. The fourth conception of cruelty and the normative model that gives it meaning seek to address these limitations. They transcend discrete agency and conscious suffering as the core definitional elements

[16] *Id.* at 1033 (*quoting Farmer v. Brennan*, 511 U.S. 825, 826, (1994)).
[17] *Id.* at 1047.
[18] *Id.* at 1033.

of cruelty. In the victim-objective/agent-independent conception of cruelty, agency is transcended by structural causation and suffering is transcended by violation of human dignity.[19]

E. International Law

International law addresses the definition of cruelty obliquely. Article 1 of the Convention against Torture and Other Cruel, Inhuman or Degrading Treatment or Punishment (commonly known as the United Nations Convention against Torture (UNCAT)) does not define "cruelty" but defines "torture" as:

> [A]ny act by which severe pain or suffering, whether physical or mental, is intentionally inflicted on a person for such purposes as obtaining from him, or a third person, information or a confession, punishing him for an act he or a third person has committed or is suspected of having committed, or intimidating or coercing him or a third person, or for any reason based on discrimination of any kind, when such pain or suffering is inflicted by or at the instigation of or with the consent or acquiescence of a public official or other person acting in an official capacity. It does not include pain or suffering arising only from, inherent in, or incidental to, lawful sanctions.[20]

Article 16 of the UNCAT prohibits "acts of cruel, inhuman or degrading treatment or punishment which do not amount to torture as defined in article 1.[21] Accordingly, from the perspective of international law, torture is a subset of cruelty.

F. U.S. Law

United States law also defines "cruelty" in different ways. As will be discussed at greater length in this essay, the Supreme Court of the United States definition of "cruelty" as set forth in

---

[19] *Id.* at 1053.
[20] Convention Against Torture and Other Cruel, Inhuman, or Degrading Treatment or Punishment, art. 1, P 1, Dec. 10, 1984, 1465 U.N.T.S. 85, https://www.refworld.org/docid/3ae6b3a94.html (last accessed Feb. 3 2022) [hereinafter Torture Convention].
[21] *Id.* at art. 16, P.1.

the Eighth Amendment to the U.S. Constitution has developed in different ways, tied to the notion of "cruel and unusual" punishment, starting with the statement that "[p]unishments are cruel when they involve torture or a lingering death; but the punishment of death is not cruel, within the meaning of that word as used in the Constitution. It implies there something inhuman and barbarous, and something more than the mere extinguishment of life."[22] Most of the Supreme Court's Eighth Amendment jurisprudence involves the concept of "evolving standards of decency."[23] Today, with its new conservative majority, the Supreme Court's Eighth Amendment jurisprudence tends to employ a more workable approach for evaluating whether a punishment is "cruel and unusual."[24]

G. Musician Nick Lowe

Musician Nick Lowe sang enigmatically about cruelty in the 1970s popular song "Cruel to be Kind" with a chorus of:

> You've gotta be cruel to be kind, in the right measure
>
> Cruel to be kind, it's a very good sign
>
> Cruel to be kind, means that I love you, baby
>
> (You've gotta be cruel)
>
> You gotta be cruel to be kind[25]

This song reminds us of a line from William Shakespeare's *Hamlet*.

H. William Shakespeare

---

[22] *See In Re Kemmler*, 136 U.S. 436, 447 (1890).
[23] *See, e.g.,Trop v. Dulles*, 356 U.S. 86, 101 (1958).
[24] *See, e.g., Jones v. Mississippi*, 141 S.Ct. 1307 (2021).
[25] NICK LOWE & IAN GOMM, *Cruel to be Kind* (Columbia Records & Radarscope Records 1979) (released as a single in both the U.S. the U.K.).

In William Shakespeare's *Hamlet*, Hamlet says: "I must be cruel only to be kind; Thus bad begins, and worse remains behind."[26] Hamlet believes that doing something harsh now (speaking brutally to his mother, exposing uncomfortable truths) is necessary to achieve a greater good later—namely, stopping deeper corruption and moral decay. He speaks essentially of "tough love." The immediate act may look bad on the surface, but by doing it, Hamlet hopes to prevent something even worse from continuing or taking hold.

I. Other Considerations

It is interesting that the definition of "cruelty" often includes the term "inhumane," as it is actually peculiarly human to be cruel.[27] Clearly, there is a relationship and antagonism between cruelty and love, and perhaps cruelty (rather than hatred) can be understood as the opposite of love. Like "obscenity," perhaps "cruelty" is also evasive of facile definition and is a "know it when you see it" type of concept.

Is it cruel to kill someone if it is done without pain or suffering to the decedent?[28] What about the potential mental anguish visited upon the decedent's family and loved ones by the killing – does that transferred pain and suffering fit the definition? If done for no good reason (i.e., not for lawful self-defense), isn't a homicide always a cruel act – regardless of whether it inflicted pain or suffering on the decedent or their friends and family? To kill someone, other than in self-defense, would seem to be the ultimate infringement upon human dignity, and therefore simply and unavoidably barbaric and cruel.

J. The Author's Definition

[26] WILLIAM SHAKESPEARE, HAMLET act 3, sc. 4, l. 180-84 (Hamlet addressing Polonius).
[27] With the possible exception of a house cat playing with and killing a mouse.
[28] *See infra* p. 27 (the government now uses the painless method of lethal injection to administer the death penalty).

None of these definitions by itself seems fully satisfactory in this difficult exercise. Synthesizing the various treatments of the subject, the essential ingredients of the cruelty recipe appear to include:

(1) the willful or intentional infliction of death or severe physical or mental pain and suffering;

(2) the willful or intentional withholding of aid to avoid death or severe physical or mental pain and suffering;

(3) done without necessity or reasonable moral justification; or done with malice or degenerate pleasure; and

(4) where the end result is regarded by a reasonable person as barbaric or violative of human dignity.

III. WHAT CAUSES CRUELTY?

While generally beyond the scope of this essay, the question of what causes a person to be cruel to another is intriguing. Of course, there are different theories. Some resort to religious explanations and the problem of evil or the necessity of suffering. Some religious traditions attribute cruelty to God. Other approaches attack the issue from the perspective of science (psychology, biology, neuroscience, etc.).

In his essay entitled The True Cause of Cruelty, The Real Reason People are Cruel to One Another, Dr. Alex Lickerman explains it from a psychological perspective:

> It's called the spirit of abstraction, a term originally coined by Gabriel Marcel in his essay "The Spirit of Abstraction as a Factor Making for War," and is defined as *the practice of conceiving of people as functions rather than as human beings*. In early American history a large segment of the population labeled African Americans as

> "slaves," reducing their identity as human beings into an abstract idea only, freeing slave owners to consider slaves their property. Hitler convinced a majority of Germans to conceive of a segment of their population as "Jews," abstracting their identity as human beings into something he convinced the German people was so inferior he was able to wipe out 6 million of them (not to mention half a million gypsies as well). Americans, in turn, abstracted the Japanese people into "Japs," a derogatory term that reduced them from human beings with hopes, loves, families, and fears into the "enemy" on whom it was therefore eventually permissible to drop two atomic bombs.[29]

Others believe the opposite is true – that humans are cruel to one another precisely because they recognize the humanity of the other person.[30] "We see other people as blameworthy, as morally responsible, as themselves cruel, as not giving us what we deserve, as taking more than they deserve. And so we treat them horribly precisely because we see them as moral human beings."[31]

If we look back to ancient Rome, one of the fundamental tenets of the Roman law was the differentiation between the slave and the free man. Slaves had essentially no rights and were treated cruelly. Likewise, the 1750 B.C. jurisprudence of the Code of Hammurabi prescribed that concerning slavery, that "if a slave should declare to his master, "You are not my master", he [the master] shall bring charge and proof against him that he is indeed his slave, and his master shall cut off his ear." We know from our own American experience that slavery and its aftermath was attended by extreme cruelty to slaves, former slaves and their progeny.

---

[29] Alex Lickerman, *The True Cause of Cruelty, The Real Reason People are Cruel to One Another*, PSYCHOLOGY TODAY (Dec. 7, 2009), https://www.psychologytoday.com/us/blog/happiness-in-world/200912/the-true-cause-cruelty.
[30] *See* Sean Illing, *Why Humans are Cruel*, VOX (Dec. 1, 2019), https://www.vox.com/science-and-health/2017/12/14/16687388/cruelty-border-immigration-psychology-human-nature.
[31] *Id.*

In all instances, objectification or abstraction of a person as a slave paved the way for cruelty. The same was true in mid-twentieth century Germany where Jews, gypsies and homosexuals, among others, we considered less than human and almost exterminated.[32]

Whatever the underlying cause of cruelty may be, it proves to be an intractable problem in our modern society, just as it has been throughout the recorded history of humankind, despite the patchwork of laws designed to prohibit it and protect against it. It is an ineffable and inescapable component of human nature to be cruel and to despise cruelty at the same time.

IV. PROGRESS OR A LACK THEREOF

Some would argue that we have not come that far since the days of the Colosseum. It is hard to evaluate whether progress has been made by Western civilization in alleviating cruelty by law. How does one measure the quantity or quality of cruelty that exists from time to time or the evolution in cruelty over time? Even with the advent of a plethora of laws prohibiting cruelty, we know that slavery, war, genocide and heinous individual acts which have marred all of human history with cruelty continue to do so.

While for the most part we no longer countenance the likes of slavery and crucifixion, the twentieth century was nonetheless marked by horrific acts of cruelty. Not to mention war itself, from the Nazi Holocaust in Europe to Pol Pot's Killing Fields of Southeast Asia, governments have engaged in industrial scale cruelty. Likewise, from the 1955 case of 14-year-old Emmett

---

[32] When I was a young schoolboy, I watched a film with my parents called *Night and Fog*. It was a 1956 French documentary short film that detailed the horrors of the Holocaust in black and white and color. That experience was perhaps my first searing brush with true cruelty. The film left an indelible mark on me and has led to a fascination on my part with the problem of "man's inhumanity to man". It is undoubtedly one of the primary reasons I was drawn to an education and career in the law.

Till, who was brutally murdered for allegedly flirting with a white woman (lynching of African Americans typically evokes images of Black men and women hanging from trees, and other extreme brutality, such as torture, mutilation, decapitation, and desecration -- some victims being burned alive), to the case of Matthew Shepard, a young gay man who was brutally tortured and beaten to death in 1998 near Laramie, Wyoming, the instances of individual cruelty in modern times are far too many to recount. We also still put people to death in the name of punishment on a somewhat regular basis in this country.

Furthermore, even the U.S. government recently got into the cruelty business (beyond capital punishment) for a short period of time. The George W. Bush administration, in the wake of the 9/11 terrorist attack, disturbingly implemented "enhanced interrogation techniques" that many considered nothing more than a euphemism for outright torture.[33] The U.S. intelligence agencies and armed services used methods on detainees such as (1) beating them, (2) binding them in contorted stress positions, (3) hooding them, (4) subjection them to deafening noise, (5) depriving them of sleep to the point of hallucination, (6) depriving them of food, drink, and medical care for wounds, as well as (7) waterboarding and "walling" them, (8) sexually humiliating them, (9) subjecting them to extreme heat or extreme cold, and (10) confining them in small coffin-like boxes.[34] Whether they constitute torture or not, and whether they violate U.S. or international law, these practices are clearly cruel.

In its defense, the Bush Administration primarily argued that this practice was necessary and justified by the need to obtain intelligence to assist in the War on Terror. However, the cruelty

[33] *See generally* S. REP. NO. 113-288 (2014) (the partially declassified U.S. Senate Select Committee on Intelligence, Committee Study of the CIA's Detention and Interrogation Program itself describes the techniques as "brutal", "abuses", and compares the techniques to "torture" over 150 times.
[34] *See generally id.*

was manifest, but the actual efficacy of these techniques was dubious at best.[35] Cruelty doesn't age well. This practice did nothing to boost our human rights credibility internationally.[36] Historian Arthur M. Schlesinger Jr. in assessing the effect of the Bush program on the international reputation of the United States, stated that the damage had been incalculable -- "No position taken has done more damage to the American reputation in the world – ever."[37] Accordingly, it was both inefficacious and counterproductive and, therefore, very difficult to justify or explain on moral grounds.

Many would argue that the Trump Administration's current mass deportation efforts constitute cruelty. Those efforts have sparked significant protests and resistance, most notably in Chicago, Illinois and Minneapolis-St. Paul, Minnesota. The unrest has recently led to the tragic deaths of two individuals resisting or interfering with Immigration and Customs Enforcement agents attempting to effect the arrest of criminal illegal aliens. On the other hand, the American voters spoke clearly and loudly in favor of this policy in the 2024 Presidential election. Perhaps it is the methods and scale of the deportation operations being implemented, the perceived targets of the operations, or the near-rabid ferocity of those operations that are most objectionable. In any event, the chaotic scenes emanating from Minnesota in January of 2026 certainly evoke a sense of cruelty, despite the government's legitimate stated purpose and justification for its policy.

V. THE UTILITY OF CRUELTY

---

[35] *See id.* at xi (finding that "the CIA's enhanced interrogation techniques was not an effective means of obtaining accurate information or gaining detainee cooperation.").

[36] *See id.* at xxv (finding that "The CIA's Detention and Interrogation Program created tensions with U.S. partners and allies, leading to formal *demarches* to the United States, and damaging and complicating bilateral intelligence relationships . . . . More broadly, the program caused immeasurable damage to the United States' public standing, as well as to the United States' longstanding global leadership on human rights in general and the prevention of torture in particular.").

[37] JANE MAYER, THE DARK SIDE: THE INSIDE STORY OF HOW THE WAR ON TERROR TURNED INTO A WAR ON AMERICAN IDEALS, 8 (Doubleday 2008).

Part of any workable definition of cruelty is the concept of lack of necessity or moral justification. That is, to be cruel, an act must generally be undertaken without necessity or reasonable moral justification. Accordingly, an act is not considered to constitute cruelty where it is necessary or morally justified, unless done with malice or degenerate pleasure. However, separate and apart from that concept, an act conceded to be unnecessary or unjustified from a moral standpoint and therefore cruel might otherwise be undertaken for utilitarian[38] ends.

For example, the cruel act, while admittedly cruel, might serve to benefit the greater good. Sometimes cruelty can be seen as a good. We find this concept in punishment that is intended to be a deterrent. To exact a penalty which is so onerous that it has a profound deterrent effect on the public, cruelty is generally required. It is still cruelty. It is just cruelty knowingly and purposefully employed to obtain a result which society believes has utility. Likewise, to convince others to avoid certain acts in the future, cruelty is required for the *in terrorem* effect. In this regard, cruelty becomes a tool of the law rather than something to be prohibited by the law.

We see the utility of cruelty exhibited in stark contrast when we examine the Supreme Court's Eighth Amendment jurisprudence regarding harsh treatment of school children to restore discipline in school and prisoners to restore order in prison. As is discussed below, the Supreme Court in *Ingraham v. Wright*[39] and *Whitley v. Albers* [40] determined that conduct by the government that would ordinarily clearly constitute cruelty was justified and therefore did not constitute cruel and unusual punishment so long as it was used in a good faith effort to restore order and discipline in a public institution.

---

[38] English Philosopher, Jeremy Bentham, founded modern utilitarianism stating that "the greatest happiness of the greatest number is the measure of right and wrong." *See* Jeremy Bentham, A COMMENT ON THE COMMENTARIES AND A FRAGMENT ON GOVERNMENT, 393 (J. H. Burns & H. L. A. Hart eds., Univ. of London: Athlone Press 1977).

[39] *See* 430 U.S. 651, 662 (1977).

[40] 475 U.S. 312, 320 (1986).

In *Ingraham*, a junior high student was beaten twenty times with a paddle while being held down in a prone position.[41] The student was later taken to a hospital for treatment, where he was prescribed cold compresses, laxatives and pain-killing medication for a hematoma.[42] In a 5-4 decision the Supreme Court held that the Eighth Amendment did not forbid this type of corporal punishment in public schools under the circumstances.[43]

In *Whitley*, a prison guard shot a prisoner in the knee with a shotgun during the course of quelling a prison riot.[44] The Supreme Court held that because the shooting was part of a good-faith effort to restore security to the prison there was insufficient evidence of wanton conduct and it did not violate the injured inmate's Eighth Amendment rights.[45]

VI. PUNISHMENT

The U.S. tends to be cruel in its administration of criminal justice, as it focuses primarily on the utilitarian principles of deterrence and incapacity and the Kantian principle of retribution in punishment. The primary goal of our criminal justice system is and should be to prevent crime, not to punish offenders. "An ounce of prevention is worth a pound of cure."[46] There is a great deal of debate over what form of punishment best achieves that goal.

There are several theories regarding methods of punishment. Rehabilitation prevents crime by altering a defendant's behavior. Retribution prevents crime by giving victims or society a feeling of avengement, a balancing of the scales, which creates a sense of justice in and of itself, but which also can stop a cycle of violence. Deterrence prevents crime by frightening the public with the punishment of a defendant thereby discouraging the public from engaging in criminal conduct.

---

[41] *Ingraham*, 430 U.S. at 657.
[42] *Ingraham v. Wright*, 498 F.2d 248, 256 (1974).
[43] *Ingraham*, 430 U.S. at 664.
[44] *Whitley*, 475 U.S. at 314-16.
[45] *Id.* at 324.
[46] Benjamin Franklin, *On Protection of Towns From Fire*, PA. GAZETTE, Feb. 4, 1735.

Incapacitation prevents crime by removing a criminal from society. Restoration serves to restore or repair justice through shared value or putting the victim back to the *status quo ante*. Punishment should attempt to strike a proper balance among these factors.

However, generally speaking, most of Western society has adopted a model of criminal justice which is weighted toward rehabilitation. That makes sense in that the best way to achieve the goal of crime prevention is through punishment that is rehabilitative in nature. Studies show that the rehabilitation model reduces recidivism whereas retribution only further acerbates the offender's antisociality and contempt for authority.[47] Rehabilitation is also a utilitarian concept and has the tendency to be less barbaric than other forms of punishment.

Among the Western nations, the U.S. currently has more of a deterrence, retributive and incapacitation model. Common restitution orders invoke the theory of restorative justice as well. The impetus behind many punishments in our system is clearly deterrence, retribution or incapacitation. Fines can be onerous. Prison sentences are more common, lengthier and the prison experience is more punitive. Many states and the federal government also utilize capital punishment, unlike many developed nations. Most nations have abolished capital punishment. We join the likes of China, India, Indonesia, Pakistan, Bangladesh, Nigeria, Egypt, Saudi Arabia, Iran, Japan, and Taiwan in retaining the practice.

Retribution seems to generally make sense. The idea of retribution appeals to the common person as righting a wrong. It *feels* like justice. It serves the base notion of revenge, or *Lex Talionis*.[48] It is founded in human nature, and particularly our nature to be cruel or to see and use cruelty as a good or as a tool. More disturbingly, it would seem that even prison rape and violence

---

47 Joan Petersilia, *Beyond the Prison Bubble*, NATIONAL INSTITUTE OF JUSTICE, (Nov. 2, 2011), https://nij.ojp.gov/topics/articles/beyond-prison-bubble

48 *Lex Talionis*: an eye for an eye, a tooth for a tooth, a life for a life.

is a *de facto* component part of retributive punishment. Attitudes toward punishment among the public include an acceptance, if not celebration, of the idea that prisoners are subjected to rape and violence by other inmates while incarcerated as just deserts. The end result of a system too weighted toward retribution, without proper regard to proportionality, can be cruelty. As we learned in kindergarten, two wrongs don't make a right.

Incapacitation also makes sense. If someone cannot follow the rules of society, they need to be removed from society. Like retribution, however, incapacitation can become cruel. A sentence that is too lengthy when compared with the crime committed can be cruel. A sentence that involves extended periods of solitary confinement is cruel. Incapacitation in the form of removing the prisoner from society by killing the prisoner is cruel.

Likewise, deterrence has its positive aspects. Nevertheless, retribution, deterrence and incapacity make no accounting for excess or cruelty.

Until the mid-1970s, rehabilitation was a key part of U.S. prison policy. The focus was on improving a prisoner's education and skills and addressing any psychological or substance abuse problems the prisoner may have. The ultimate goal was to prepare the prisoner to perform well in society as a productive citizen once freed. This was thought to reduce the likelihood of the prisoner reoffending.

Since then, however, the concept of deterrence, retribution and incapacity have substantially replaced rehabilitation, as our society has determined to "get tough on crime." The new approach has created explosive growth in the prison population. Between 1973 and 1990, the American prison population tripled.[49] The "war on drugs" has substantially contributed to this. The U.S. imprisons more people per capita (approximately 629 per 100,000) than any other

[49] Melvin Gutterman, *The Contours of Eighth Amendment Prison Jurisprudence: Conditions of Confinement*, 48 SMU L. Rev. 373, 374 (1995).

country in the world.[50] At the other end of the spectrum is Norway which has one of the lowest rates, at approximately 56 per 100,000.[51]

There is scant evidence that this change in punishment philosophy has had a meaningful impact on crime rates. On the other hand, it has definitely introduced more cruelty into the criminal justice system.

The American model seems to be more utilitarian in nature. It looks at achieving the greatest good for the greatest number through deterrence of crime rather than focusing on the issues of cruelty. It pays less attention to Kantian moral theory based upon respecting persons as ends in themselves rather than means alone. It also ignores Libertarianism, which also places primary value upon the individual's rather than society's interests. Hegel objects to this utilitarian model focused on deterrence saying: "To base a justification of punishment on threat is to liken it to the act of a man who lifts his stick to a dog. It is to treat a man like a dog instead of with freedom and respect due to him as a man."[52] On the other hand, the retributive nature of the modern U.S. system does draw from the concept of just deserts – a Kantian notion of punishment. A more balanced approach to punishment, as espoused by John Rawls[53] (combining the Kantian and Utilitarian views) with an eye to avoiding cruelty, would be more appropriate if the goal was to reduce the level of cruelty in society.

---

[50]INST. FOR CRIME & JUST. POL'Y, RSCH., *World Prison Brief Data, U.S.*, https://www.prisonstudies.org/country/united-states-america (last visited Feb. 2, 2022).
[51]INST. FOR CRIME & JUST. POL'Y, RSCH., *World Prison Brief Data, Norway*, https://www.prisonstudies.org/country/norway (last visited Feb. 2, 2022).
[52] G.W.F HEGEL, HEGEL'S PHILOSOPHY OF RIGHT, 246 (1942).
[53] An American political philosopher whose theory of justice as fairness describes a society of free citizens holding equal basic rights and cooperating within an egalitarian economic system.

VII. U.S. LAW PROHIBITING GOVERNMENT CRUEL AND UNUSUAL PUNISHMENT – THE EIGHTH AMENDMENT

As the Eighth Amendment jurisprudence of the United States Supreme Court has a substantial bearing on our society's concept of cruelty, a brief outline of that jurisprudence is warranted here. The jurisprudence covered here includes punishments from death (and the conditions surrounding it), to life in prison without parole, torture and prison overcrowding. This examination exposes concepts of cruelty at play in punishment over the past 3 centuries in the United States and England. It gives us a sense of how the law attempts to address cruelty in the context of punishment.

Modern U.S. law prohibits the government from imposing "cruel and unusual" punishment. It does not prohibit punishment that is cruel *although usual*. Adopted in 1791 as part of the original Bill of Rights, the Eighth Amendment to the United States Constitution states: "Excessive bail shall not be required, nor excessive fines imposed, nor cruel and unusual punishments inflicted."[54]

The principles underlying this law have their origin in England's Bill of Rights, including its declaration against "cruel and unusual punishments" approved by Parliament in 1689. The declaration may have in some part been the result of the English case of Titus Oates who, in 1685, was tried for multiple acts of perjury that had led to executions of many people Oates had wrongly accused. Oates was sentenced to imprisonment, including an annual ordeal of being taken out for two days of pillory plus one day of whipping while tied to a moving cart.

[54] U.S. CONST. amend. VIII.

In 1776, George Mason included a prohibition of cruel and unusual punishments in the Declaration of Rights he drafted for the Commonwealth of Virginia. In 1791, this same prohibition became the central component of the Eighth Amendment to the United States Constitution.

In 1878, the United States Supreme Court in *Wilkerson v. Utah*[55] held that the Eighth Amendment forbids "punishments of torture, ... and all others in the same line of unnecessary cruelty," such as disemboweling, beheading, quartering, dissecting, and burning alive, all of which share the deliberate infliction of pain for the sake of pain.

Later in 1910, the United States Supreme Court, in *Weems v. United States*[56], ruled on a case in which a Philippine court, having convicted a customs official of falsifying a public document, imposed a sentence of fifteen years in which the offender was to be chained around his ankles and wrists for the entirety of his prison term. It was not a capital case. The Court in Weems struck down the sentence on Eighth Amendment grounds. There is language in the opinion suggesting that the punishment was unconstitutional because of its barbarity.[57] Additionally, other language suggests that the punishment was improper because it was not proportioned to the offense.[58] So with *Weems*, we get the concepts of barbarity and proportionality in defining "cruel and unusual."

To be blunt, Eighth Amendment jurisprudence following *Weems* devolves into virtual nonsense, beginning with the 1958 case of *Trop v. Dulles*.[59] In *Trop*, not a capital case either, the Court's Chief Justice Earl Warren stated: "The [Eighth] Amendment must draw its meaning from

---

[55] 99 U.S. 130, 135-36 (1878).
[56] 217 U.S. 349 (1910).
[57] *See id.* at 366 ("No circumstance of degradation is omitted. It may be that even the cruelty of pain is not omitted. He must bear a chain night and day. He is condemned to painful as well as hard labor. What painful labor may mean we have no exact measure.").
[58] *See id.* at 380–81.
[59] 356 U.S. 86 (1958).

the evolving standards of decency that mark the progress of a maturing society."[60] What that means is anyone's guess. It is certainly not a standard which can be consistently applied. This statement has become the basis for the concept of a living Constitution. The Courts have struggled with this concept ever since, leading to fractious opinions and significant divisions within the Court.

Trop, an Army private stationed in Casablanca in 1944, was sentenced to the stockade for a breach of discipline.[61] He escaped and wandered along a road toward Rabat.[62] Growing increasingly tired, cold and hungry, and without any money, Trop returned to the stockade within less than a day.[63] A general court martial found him guilty of desertion and sentenced him to three years of hard labor.[64] Trop served his prison term and, in 1952, applied for a passport.[65] The State Department rejected his application, finding that he had lost his citizenship, pursuant to a Civil War statute, by virtue of his conviction for desertion.[66] Trop filed suit seeking a declaration that he was still a citizen.[67] A district court denied his petition, and a divided panel of the Second Circuit United States Court of Appeals affirmed.[68] Trop appealed to the Supreme Court where he challenged the constitutionality of that decision on two grounds.[69] Important here was the argument that the imposition of denationalization as a punishment in his case violated the Eighth Amendment.

---

[60] *Id.* at 101.
[61] *Id. at* 87.
[62] *Id.*
[63] *Id.*
[64] *Id.* at 88.
[65] *Id.*
[66] *Id.*
[67] *Id.*
[68] *Id.*
[69] *See id.* at 91-92, 94 (Trop argued both that citizenship could not be revoked via court-martial and that even if it could denationalization may not be inflicted as a punishment).

The Supreme Court held in Trop's favor.[70] Chief Justice Warren announced that "[t]he basic concept underlying the Eighth Amendment is nothing less than the dignity of man."[71] In crafting the majority opinion, Chief Justice Warren drew on four sources: his own moral intuitions (his "faith"), the opinions of the "civilized nations of the world" (as reflected in U.N. documents), academic literature (including law review student notes), and "widely accepted" American practice.[72] Here we have a moving subjective target concept for the definition of cruel and unusual.

Justice Frankfurter dissented arguing that in attempting to discern the "evolving standards of decency" the criteria would be so open-ended that the judicial power would be immeasurably expanded.[73] The late Justice Scalia, an originalist, later took issue with *Trop* and this notion of an evolving meaning of Constitutional language.[74] In two cases in the last decade of Justice Scalia's life, *Baze v. Rees* and *Glossip v. Gross*, the Court considered challenges to the constitutionality of the three-drug execution protocol. In both cases, Justice Scalia joined the concurring opinions of Justice Thomas, who concluded that the original meaning of the Eighth Amendment was to foreclose only those punishments that are "deliberately designed to inflict pain."[75] Here we have the concept of intentional infliction of pain and suffering as the definition of cruel and unusual.

Subsequent to *Trop*, the Supreme Court looked to societal developments and its own independent judgment in determining what are those "evolving standards of decency". In terms of capital punishment, most of the states and the federal government impose the death penalty for certain criminal offenses. All such states and the federal government now use the lethal injection

---

[70] *Id.* at 103.
[71] *Id.* at 100.
[72] *See id.* at 96 n.18, 99, 101 n.33, 103.
[73] *See id.* at 100, 119.
[74] *See* Craig S. Lerner, *Justice Scalia's Eighth Amendment Jurisprudence: The Failure of Sake-of-Argument Originalism*, HARV. J. of L. & PUB. POL'Y, Vol. 42, No. 1 (2019).
[75] *Baze v. Rees*, 553 U.S. 35, 94 (2008) (Thomas, J., concurring); *see also Glossip v. Gross*, 576 U.S. 863, 899 (2015) (Thomas, J., concurring).

method. Under the 2008 case of *Baze v. Rees*[76] and the 2015 case of *Glossip v. Gross*,[77] the United States Supreme Court has held that the use of lethal injection to kill prisoners convicted of capital crimes does not constitute cruel and unusual punishment.

In the 1972 case of *Furman v. Georgia,*[78] Justice Brennan wrote, "There are, then, four principles by which we may determine whether a particular punishment is 'cruel and unusual'."

- The "essential predicate" is "that a punishment must not by its severity be degrading to human dignity," especially torture.[79]
- "A severe punishment that is obviously inflicted in wholly arbitrary fashion."[80]
- "A severe punishment that is clearly and totally rejected throughout society."[81]
- "A severe punishment that is patently unnecessary."[82]

Justice Brennan added:

> The function of these principles, after all, is simply to provide [the] means by which a court can determine whether [the] challenged punishment comports with human dignity. They are, therefore, interrelated, and, in most cases, it will be their convergence that will justify the conclusion that a punishment is 'cruel and unusual'. The test, then, will ordinarily be a cumulative one: if a punishment is unusually severe, if there is a strong probability that it is inflicted arbitrarily, if it is substantially rejected by contemporary society, and if there is no reason to believe that it serves any penal purpose more effectively than some less severe punishment, then the continued infliction of that punishment violates the command of the Clause that the State may not inflict inhuman and uncivilized punishments upon those convicted of crimes.[83]

[76] 553 U.S. 35 (2008).
[77] 576 U.S. 863 (2015).
[78] 408 U.S. 238, 281 (1972).
[79] *Id.*
[80] *Id.*
[81] *Id.*
[82] *Id.*
[83] *Id.* at 282.

The *Furman* decision invalidated all death penalty schemes in the United States in a 5–4 decision, with each member of the majority writing a separate opinion. The case holding was that the arbitrary and inconsistent imposition of the death penalty in three cases violates the Eighth and Fourteenth Amendments and constitutes cruel and unusual punishment. It mandated a degree of consistency in the application of the death penalty. This case resulted in a *de facto* moratorium of capital punishment throughout the United States, which ended when the case *Gregg v. Georgia*[84] was decided in 1976 to once again allow the death penalty.

The issue of capital punishment has been a mainstay at the Supreme Court over the past few decades. In the 1986 case of *Ford v. Wainwright*,[85] the Court upheld the common law rule that the insane cannot be executed. In 1988, the Supreme Court ruled in *Thompson v. Oklahoma* that mere deterrence is not a valid reason for a jury or judge to sentence a 15-year-old juvenile to the death penalty.[86] In a 1989 5-to-4 decision the Supreme Court in *Stanford v. Kentucky* held that in weighing whether the imposition of capital punishments on offenders below the age of eighteen is cruel and unusual, it is necessary to look at the given society's evolving decency standards.[87]

What evolving standards of decency? Can it be said that we are a more evolved, enlightened and decent society today than we were 200 years ago? How about 2000 years ago? Do we take polls to make this determination? How is this measured? Isn't that a legislative function rather than a judicial one? The standard is very practical and not principled. It involves nine justices, the identity of whom will differ from time to time, simply exercising their own independent judgment of whether a particular fact scenario can support the imposition of capital punishment. The United

[84] 428 U.S. 153 (1976).
[85] 477 U.S. 399 (1986).
[86] *Thompson v. Oklahoma*, 487 U.S. 815, 830 (1988).
[87] *Stanford v. Kentucky*, 492 U.S. 361, 370 n.1 (1989).

States Supreme Court, while historically very divided on the appropriate approach, takes the view that the societal standards in this regard have evolved and that they are discernable by the courts.

In 2002, the Supreme Court, in a 6-3 decision, ruled that executions of mentally retarded criminals are "cruel and unusual punishments" prohibited by the Eighth Amendment.[88] In 2005, the U.S. Supreme Court ruled that that the Eighth and Fourteenth Amendments forbid the execution of offenders who were younger than age 18 when the crime occurred. The vote was 5-4.[89] The Supreme Court decided that a court may refer "to the laws of other countries and to international authorities as instructive for its interpretation of the Eighth Amendment's prohibition of cruel and unusual punishments."[90] As these rulings make clear, courts have "consistently referred to foreign and international law as relevant to [their] assessment of evolving standards of decency."[91]

In the 2008 case of *Kennedy v. Louisiana*, the Supreme Court stated: "Evolving standards of decency must embrace and express respect for the dignity of the person, and the punishment of criminals must conform to that rule."[92] The Court held that the Eighth Amendment's Cruel and Unusual Punishments Clause prohibits imposing the death penalty for the rape of a child in cases where the victim did not die and death was not intended.[93] In the 1977 Supreme Court case of

[88] *Atkins v. Virginia*, 536 U.S. 304, 317 (2002).
[89] *Roper v. Simmons*, 543 U.S. 551, 574-75 (2005).
[90] *Id.* at 575; *see also Atkins* 536 U.S. at 317 (examining international community's rejection of death penalty for persons with mental retardation); *Stanford* 492 U.S. at 370 n.1 (1989) (Scalia, J.) (stating that "the practices of other nations, particularly other democracies, can be relevant to determining whether a practice uniform among our people is not merely an historical accident, but rather so implicit in the concept of ordered liberty that it occupies a place not merely in our mores, but, text permitting, in our Constitution as well"); *Thompson* 487 U.S. at 830 (Stevens, J., concurring) (noting global rejection of the death penalty for youth offenders age sixteen or younger); Trop v. Dulles, 356 U.S. 86, 102 (1958) (finding a "virtual unanimity" within international community that denationalization constituted cruel and unusual punishment).
[91] *Roper* 543 U.S. at 604 (2005) (O'Connor, dissenting).
[92] 554 U.S. 407, 420 (2008).
[93] *Id.* at 421.

Coker v. Georgia,[94] the Court had held that the death penalty for rape of an adult woman was grossly disproportionate and excessive punishment, and therefore unconstitutional under the Eighth Amendment to the U.S. Constitution.

Keep in mind that the Eighth Amendment proscribes cruel *and unusual* punishment, not just cruel punishment. Accordingly, it does not prohibit forms of punishment which are merely cruel but usual. As such, were a usual practice cruel (i.e., killing someone for the sake of punishment), then arguably it would constitute cruelty but not run afoul of the Eighth Amendment. Justices Stevens and Breyer take the view that capital punishment in any form might be unconstitutional.[95]

"The Supreme Court has become the barometer of society's standards of decency but has failed to delineate the variables. To a great extent the Court speculates upon the societal view and this, of course, invites the Justices to project personal predilections."[96]

With regard to the punishment of imprisonment, and the proportionality of a sentence, *Harmelin v. Michigan*,[97] was a non-capital case decided by the Supreme Court under the Eighth Amendment in 1991. The Court ruled that the Eighth Amendment's Cruel and Unusual Punishment Clause allowed a state to impose a life sentence without the possibility of parole for the possession of 672 grams of cocaine.[98] *Harmelin* overturned the 1983 Supreme Court decision in *Solem v. Helm* which had held a sentence may not be disproportionate to the crime and to measure proportionality the Court was to look at (1) the severity of the offense, (2) the harshness of the

---

[94] 433 U.S. 584 (1977).
[95] *See Glossip v. Gross*, 576 U.S. 863, 893 (2015) (Scalia, J., concurring); *Baze v. Rees*, 553 U.S. 35, 87 (Scalia, J., concurring).
[96] *Gutterman, supra* note 50, at 404.
[97] 501 U.S. 957.
[98] *Id.* at 1009.

penalty, (3) the sentences imposed on others within the same jurisdiction, and (4) the sentences imposed on others in different jurisdictions.[99] *Harmelin* was followed in 2003 by *Lockyer v. Andrade*[100]which held that a gross proportionality requirement is only available in exceedingly rare and extreme cases.

Concerning age and the penalty of imprisonment, the Eighth Amendment does consider the age of the defendant in determining whether a sentence passes muster. In *Graham v. Florida*[101] and *Miller v. Alabama*[102] the Supreme Court found it unconstitutional for the state to sentence a juvenile offender (whether convicted of homicide or non-homicide offenses) to life in prison without parole.

On the subject of torture or beatings inflicted upon a prisoner, the Supreme Court has held that "unnecessary and wanton infliction of pain" violates the Eighth Amendment but only where it is not done in a good faith effort to restore discipline rather than done maliciously to cause harm.[103] Applying this standard, the Court in *Hope v. Pelzer*[104] found that a prisoner who was handcuffed to a hitching post for seven hours, taunted and denied bathroom facilities had been treated in a cruel and unusual manner in violation of the Eighth Amendment. Also, in *Hudson v. McMillian*[105] the Court determined that the state of mind of the prison guards and not the lack of significant injury to the prisoner was the key to violation of the Eighth Amendment, and where the guards acted maliciously and sadistically the punishment would be cruel and unusual even though the prisoner did not experience significant injury.

---

[99] 463 U.S. 277, 292 (1983).
[100] 538 U.S. 63 (2003).
[101] 560 U.S. 48 (2010).
[102] 567 U.S. 460 (2012).
[103] *See Ingraham v. Wright*, 430 U.S. 651 (1977); see *also Whitley v. Albers*, 475 U.S. 312 (1986).
[104] 536 U.S. 730 (2002).
[105] 503 U.S. 1 (1992).

With regard to prison conditions, the Supreme Court held in *Estelle v. Gamble*[106] that a prison guard's deliberate indifference to a prisoner's serious illness or injury constituted a violation of the Eighth Amendment, and in *Brown v. Plata*[107] the Court tackled the subject of prison overcrowding (prison population at almost double capacity) holding that certain living conditions were so dangerous that prisoners did not receive adequate medical care, constituting cruel and unusual punishment.

VIII. PROTECTIONS AGAINST CRUELTY IN THE FOURTH, FIFTH AND FOURTEENTH AMENDMENTS TO THE CONSTITUTION

Cruelty is also prohibited by other amendments to the Constitution. The U.S. courts have located constitutional protections against interrogations under torture in the Fourth Amendment's right to be free of unreasonable search or seizure (which encompasses the right not be abused by the police), the Fifth Amendment's right against self-incrimination (which encompasses the right to remain silent during interrogations), the Fifth and the Fourteenth Amendments' guarantees of due process (ensuring fundamental fairness in criminal justice system), in addition to the Eighth Amendment's right to be free of cruel or unusual punishment.

In numerous cases, the U.S. Supreme Court has condemned the use of force amounting to torture or other forms of ill treatment during interrogations, including such practices as whipping, slapping, depriving a victim of food, water, or sleep, keeping him naked or in a small cell for prolonged periods, holding a gun to his head, or threatening him with mob violence. Torture would also violate state constitutions, whose provisions generally parallel the protections set forth in the federal Bill of Rights.

---

[106] 429 U.S. 97 (1976).
[107] 563 U.S. 493 (2011).

The Fourth Amendment's prohibition of unreasonable searches and seizures includes a seizure, or arrest or detention, of one's person. The Fourth Amendment is one of the most important amendments in the Bill of Rights protecting people in the United States from government abuse of power. The Fourth Amendment is made applicable to the states through the Fourteenth Amendment. This law protects against certain forms of state-sponsored cruelty. The Fifth and the Fourteenth Amendments guaranty of due process of law also form a bulwark of protection against state-sponsored cruelty in the justice system, prohibiting the torture of *Kafkaesque* trials and proceedings.[108]

IX. PROTECTION BY THE FIRST AMENDMENT OF DEPICTIONS OF CRUELTY

Sometimes art and the depiction of cruelty in the form of art (films, music, literature, etc.) can have such an impact on the observer that it could be considered cruelty. This expression, however, is solidly protected against government censorship by the First Amendment to the Constitution until and unless it constitutes obscenity or defamation.[109] From a societal perspective, Tipper Gore[110] aside, we don't typically view depictions of cruelty as cruel in and of themselves.

Of course, that is not the case with child pornography, however, which violates the law. Neither does the First Amendment protect child pornography as free expression.[111]

---

[108] Franz Kafka was a German-speaking Bohemian novelist and short-story writer. One of Kafka's best known works, *The Trial,* was published posthumously in 1925. It is a dark parody of the legal system and tells the story of Josef K., a man arrested, prosecuted and executed by a remote, inaccessible authority, with the nature of his crime being unrevealed to him or the reader.

[109] *See Miller v. California*, 413 U.S. 15 (1973); *but see New York Times v. Sullivan*, 376 U.S. 254 (1964) (holding that the First Amendment protects newspapers even when they print false statements, as long as the newspapers did not act with "actual malice.").

[110] Mary Elizabeth Aitcheson Gore ("Tipper") led a successful fight in the 1980s to have parental warning labels placed on record albums that contained sexually explicit lyrics, portrayed excessive violence, or glorified drugs, and she campaigned to provide information about explicit material in music videos, television shows, and videos.

[111] *New York v. Ferber*, 458 U.S. 747 (1982).

We tend to have a tough exterior when it comes to art, and it is hard to imagine too many instances in which art would be considered cruelty. However, our culture is changing in this regard. While art is becoming aggressively disturbing, there is also a newfound focus on avoiding triggers for those with particular sensitivities to controversial speech and art. This is a dangerous trend as it tends to undermine the marketplace of ideas concept which has been responsible in large part for the success of our experiment in republican government. Often the antidote to this form of cruelty is simply "growing a thicker skin."

X. INTERNATIONAL LAW REGARDING CRUELTY

There is an absolute ban on torture and other cruel, inhuman or degrading treatment and outrages upon personal dignity under international humanitarian law and international human rights law.

The Convention against Torture and Other Cruel, Inhuman or Degrading Treatment or Punishment (commonly known as the United Nations Convention against Torture (UNCAT)) is an international human rights treaty, under the review of the United Nations, that aims to prevent torture and other acts of cruel, inhuman, or degrading treatment or punishment around the world.[112] Article 16 requires parties to prevent "other acts of cruel, inhuman or degrading treatment or punishment which do not amount to torture as defined in article 1."[113] The United States is a signatory.

The text of the Convention was adopted by the United Nations General Assembly in 1984 and, following ratification by the 20th state party, it came into force on in 1987.[114] Since the

---

[112] Torture Convention, *supra* note 22.
[113] Torture Convention, *supra* note 22, art. 16, P 1,
[114] Haus Danelius, *Convention Against Torture and Other Cruel, Inhuman, or Degrading Treatment or Punishment*, AUDIOVISUAL LIBR. OF INT'L L. (June 2008), https://legal.un.org/avl/ha/catcidtp/catcidtp.html.

convention's entry into force, the absolute prohibition against torture and other acts of cruel, inhuman, or degrading treatment or punishment has become accepted as a principle of customary international law. The Convention has 173 state parties.[115] The U.S. has been a signatory since 1988, with certain reservations.[116]

The Geneva Conventions are rules that inform countries at war how to treat wounded and captured enemy forces and enemy civilians.[117] They were signed in Geneva, Switzerland, by representatives of many countries between 1864 and 1949.[118] They are rules that apply only in times of armed conflict and seek to protect people who are not or are no longer taking part in hostilities.[119] These protections include the sick and wounded of armed forces on the field, wounded, sick, and shipwrecked members of armed forces at sea, prisoners of war, and civilians.[120] The first convention dealt with the treatment of wounded and sick armed forces in the field.[121] The second convention dealt with the sick, wounded, and shipwrecked members of armed forces at sea.[122] The third convention dealt with the treatment of prisoners of war during times of conflict.[123] The fourth convention dealt with the treatment of civilians and their protection during wartime.[124] Article 87, third paragraph, of the 1949 Geneva Convention III provides: "Any form of torture or cruelty is forbidden."[125]

---

[115] *Convention Against Torture and Other Cruel, Inhuman, or Degrading Treatment or Punishment*, U.N. TREATY COLLECTION (Feb. 24, 2022, 10:15 PM) [hereinafter UNCAT Status], https://treaties.un.org/Pages/ViewDetails.aspx?src=IND&mtdsg_no=IV-9&chapter=4&clang=_en.
[116] *Id.*
[117] Malcolm Shaw, *Geneva Conventions*, ENCYC. BRITANNICA, https://www.britannica.com/event/Geneva-Conventions/additional-info#history (Nov. 30, 2021).
[118] *Id.*
[119] *Id.*
[120] *Id.*
[121] *Id.*
[122] *Id.*
[123] *Id.*
[124] *Id.*
[125] Geneva Convention Relative to the Treatment of Prisoners of War, art. 87, Aug. 12, 1949, 75 U.N.T.S. 135.

In 1948, following the horrific abuses of World War II, the General Assembly of the United Nations inserted the prohibition against torture in the landmark Universal Declaration of Human Rights.[126] Article 5 states: "No one shall be subjected to torture or to cruel, inhuman or degrading treatment or punishment."[127] This ban on torture and other ill-treatment has subsequently been incorporated into the extensive network of international and regional human rights treaties. It is contained in Article 7 of the International Covenant on Civil and Political Rights (ICCPR)[128], with 173 party countries, including the United States which signed in 1992[129], and in the UNCAT.[130] It is also codified in the European Convention for the Protection of Human Rights and Fundamental Freedoms[131], the African Charter on Human and Peoples' Rights[132], and the American Convention on Human Rights.[133]

The Convention against Torture defines torture as "any act by which severe pain or suffering, whether physical or mental, is intentionally inflicted on a person for such purposes as obtaining from him or a third person information or a confession."[134]

XI. STATE-SPONSORED CRUELTY

Many U.S. states recognize death as a form of punishment. Some states have banned the practice, but many still subscribe to this. Of course, the legal debate is whether this form of punishment is cruel and unusual, primarily within the meaning of the federal Constitution. Usually

---

[126] *See* G.A. Res. 217 (III) A, Universal Declaration of Human Rights (Dec. 10, 1948).
[127] *Id.* art. 5
[128] G.A. Res. 2200 (XXI) A, art. 7, International Covenant on Civil and Political Rights (Dec. 16, 1966).
[129] *International Covenant on Civil and Political Rights*, U.N. TREATY COLLECTION (Feb. 25, 2022, 12:17 AM), https://treaties.un.org/Pages/ViewDetails.aspx?chapter=4&clang=_en&mtdsg_no=IV-4&src=IND.
[130] Torture Convention, *supra* note 22.
[131] Convention for the Protection of Human Rights and Fundamental Freedoms art. 3, Nov. 4, 1950, E.T.S. No. 5.
[132] *See* African Charter on Human and Peoples' Rights, art. 5, June 27, 1981, 1520 U.N.T.S 217.
[133] American Convention on Human Rights "Pact of San José, Costa Rica", art. 5, Nov. 22, 1969, 1144 U.N.T.S. 123.
[134] Torture Convention, *supra* note 22, art. 1.

implemented to punish those found guilty of cruel acts themselves, the state will take retribution by killing the convicted defendant. The punishment is said to serve the interest of retribution, deterrence and incapacity. While the death penalty in the abstract has not been found by the Supreme Court to constitute a cruel and unusual punishment, the focus instead turns to the methods and manner in which the state imposes the sentence. Many believe that the death penalty is cruel under any circumstances, and it is hard to fathom that in a just and enlightened society the death penalty still exists. But it does, despite the "evolving standards of decency" referred to by the Supreme Court in its Eighth Amendment jurisprudence.

XII. U.S. LAW PROHIBITING CRUELTY BY INDIVIDUALS

As a society, we have adopted a myriad of laws, both common law and statutory law, attempting to curb cruelty. From criminal law, to tort law (i.e., the common law tort of intentional infliction of emotional distress) and dissolution of marriage laws establishing mental or physical cruelty as grounds for divorce, we have targeted private cruelty as something abhorrent to society and which should be eliminated.

XIII. IMMIGRATION LAW

Even immigration law touches on the subject of cruelty. The Violence Against Women Act, at 8 U.S.C.A. § 1229b, provides in part:

> The Attorney General may cancel removal of, and adjust to the status of an alien lawfully admitted for permanent residence, an alien who is inadmissible or deportable from the United States if the alien demonstrates that--
> (i)(I) the alien has been battered or subjected to extreme cruelty by a spouse or parent who is or was a United States citizen (or is the parent of a child of a United States citizen and the child has been battered or subjected to extreme cruelty by such citizen parent);
> (II) the alien has been battered or subjected to extreme cruelty by a spouse or parent who is or was a lawful permanent resident (or is the parent of a child of an alien

who is or was a lawful permanent resident and the child has been battered or subjected to extreme cruelty by such permanent resident parent); or
(III) the alien has been battered or subjected to extreme cruelty by a United States citizen or lawful permanent resident whom the alien intended to marry, but whose marriage is not legitimate because of that United States citizen's or lawful permanent resident's bigamy; (Emphasis added).

While the Violence Against Women Act does not define "extreme cruelty", the Courts have stated: "Congress clearly intended extreme cruelty to indicate nonphysical aspects of domestic violence."[135] Furthermore, the federal regulations implementing the Act provide that the following constitutes extreme cruelty:

> (vi) Battery or extreme cruelty. For the purpose of this chapter, the phrase "was battered by or was the subject of extreme cruelty" includes, but is not limited to, being the victim of any act or threatened act of violence, including any forceful detention, which results or threatens to result in physical or mental injury. Psychological or sexual abuse or exploitation, including rape, molestation, incest (if the victim is a minor), or forced prostitution shall be considered acts of violence. Other abusive actions may also be acts of violence under certain circumstances, including acts that, in and of themselves, may not initially appear violent but that are a part of an overall pattern of violence. The qualifying abuse must have been committed by the citizen or lawful permanent resident spouse, must have been perpetrated against the self-petitioner or the self-petitioner's child, and must have taken place during the self-petitioner's marriage to the abuser.[136]

XIV. CRIMINAL LAW

State and local criminal laws prohibit cruelty in many forms. Criminal assault, battery, sexual assault, homicide, kidnapping, cyberbullying, extortion, domestic violence, harassment, stalking and other criminal provisions are aimed at protecting people from cruel behavior. While federal criminal law is more limited in scope, there are a number of federal statutes allowing the federal government to bring criminal charges against defendants for cruel behavior. Not every violent

---

[135] *Hernandez v. Ashcroft*, 345 F.3d 824 (9th Cir. 2003).
[136] 8 C.F.R. § 204.2(c)(1)(vi) (2007).

crime may be classified as a federal offense, and typically the offenses that the FBI and other federal agencies investigate are those involving serial murderers or serial rapists, kidnapping, and organized crime. Hate crimes, terrorist threats and charges and gang violence are other areas in which federal investigators and prosecutors may become involved. One example is the federal Matthew Shepard and James Byrd Jr. Hate Crimes Prevention Act[137], which allows the federal government to prosecute hate crimes, including those based on sexual orientation and gender identity.

XV. STATE TORT LAW

The tort laws in all states protect individuals from certain forms of cruelty, including causes of action for assault and battery, wrongful death, false imprisonment and invasion of privacy. Most states' common law of torts includes a cause of action for intentional infliction of emotional distress. This claim essentially seeks redress for mental cruelty. In *Van Stan v. Fancy Colours & Co.*, the 7th Circuit United States Court of Appeals explained the elements of the tort of intentional infliction of emotional distress in Illinois, stating:

> Under Illinois law, … a plaintiff may recover damages for intentional infliction of emotional distress only if he establishes that (1) the defendant's conduct was extreme and outrageous, (2) the defendant intended to inflict severe emotional distress or knew that there was at least a high probability that his conduct would inflict severe emotional distress, and (3) the defendant's conduct did cause severe emotional distress. *Harriston v. Chicago Tribune Co.,* 992 F.2d 697, 702 (7th Cir.1993) (quoting *McGrath v. Fahey,* 126 Ill.2d 78, 127 Ill.Dec. 724, 727, 533 N.E.2d 806, 809 (Ill.1988)). Conduct is extreme and outrageous only if "the conduct has been so outrageous in character and so extreme in degree, as to go beyond all possible bounds of decency...." *Id.* at 702–03 (quoting *Public Fin. Corp. v. Davis,* 66 Ill.2d 85, 4 Ill.Dec. 652, 654, 360 N.E.2d 765, 767 (Ill.1976)). "[M]ere insults, indignities, threats, annoyances, petty oppressions, or other trivialities" do not amount to extreme and outrageous conduct, nor does conduct "characterized by malice or a degree of aggravation which would entitle the plaintiff to punitive damages for another tort." *Public Fin. Corp.,* 4 Ill.Dec. at 654, 360 N.E.2d at 767.

---

[137] 18 U.S.C. § 249; *see also* 18 U.S.C. § 245(b)(2).

> Moreover, we judge whether conduct is extreme and outrageous on an objective standard based on all the facts and circumstances of a particular case. *Harriston,* 992 F.2d at 703; *McGrath,* 127 Ill.Dec. at 729, 533 N.E.2d at 811. Thus, to serve as a basis for recovery, the defendant's conduct must be such that the "recitation of facts to an average member of the community would arouse his resentment against the actor, and lead him to exclaim 'Outrageous!'" *Doe v. Calumet City,* 161 Ill.2d 374, 204 Ill.Dec. 274, 283, 641 N.E.2d 498, 507 (Ill.1994) (quoting Restatement (Second) of Torts § 46 cmt. d (1965)).[138]

Punitive damages are generally made available in tort cases where the element of maliciousness, willful and wanton or intentional conduct is present. Thus, enhanced damages awarded to punish rather than make whole, are designed to deter cruel conduct.

XVI. STATE DIVORCE LAW

Historically, many states' dissolution of marriage laws allowed cruelty to serve as grounds for a divorce. More recently, state law has been moving to no-fault grounds and thereby doing away with the concept of spousal cruelty.[139] That said, some states[140] still require fault grounds, and an analysis of cruelty grounds is therefore warranted. About two-thirds of the states allow a spouse the alternative to establish fault grounds for a divorce.

In New Jersey for example, one of the fault grounds for divorce is "physical or mental cruelty which endangers the safety or health of one spouse, or makes it improper or unreasonable to expect that spouse to continue to live with the abuser."[141]

---

[138] 125 F.3d 563, 567 (7th Cir. 1997).

[139] In 2016, Illinois abolished fault divorce, so spouses can no longer cite any fault grounds as the reason for their divorce. Historically extreme and repeated physical or mental cruelty was one of the fault grounds.

[140] Fault states for divorce are Alabama, Alaska, Arizona (covenant marriage), Arkansas, Connecticut, Delaware, Georgia, Maryland, New Jersey, North Carolina, South Carolina, Vermont, and Virginia. The District of Columbia also has fault divorce.

[141] N.J. STAT. ANN. § 2A:34-2 (West 2022).

XVII. HOW DOES CRUELTY MANIFEST ITSELF IN SOCIETY TODAY IN WAYS THAT ARE LEGAL?

A. Is Capital Punishment Cruel?

Capital punishment, the taking of a person's life for the sake of punishment, is cruel in the minds of many. Much has been written on this subject, and this essay does not attempt to tackle the subject comprehensively. Nevertheless, whether or not it is usual, wise or utilitarian, it meets the definition laid out herein for cruelty but only if you accept that retribution is not a proper moral justification.

It results in death, and it involves the willful infliction of pain and suffering on a person (either the decedent or their friends and family).

Is it morally justified? Deterrence is not a moral justification, even according to the Supreme Court.[142] While it may serve a utilitarian purpose, it is not a moral justification in and of itself. Is the principle of retribution a moral justification? Kant would tend to support the notion that retribution is a moral justification.[143] The question then becomes whether the punishment is proportionate – it would be unjust to punish a wrongdoer more than they deserved, and the punishment must be proportionate to the gravity of the wrong.[144] In the case of homicide, the death penalty would seem to be proportionate. The taking of the convict's life mirrors the serious crime and signals the importance of the life taken by the convict.

The death penalty certainly leaves no room for mercy or rehabilitation. Neither does it serve restoration.

---

142 *Thompson v. Oklahoma*, 487 U.S. 815, 830 (1988).
143 *See* IMMANUEL KANT, THE PHILOSOPHY OF LAW 195-201 (W. Hastie trans., Edinburgh: T. & T. Clark 1887).
144 *See* Aristotle.

It would seem to be axiomatically barbaric -- taking a human life in cold blood (whether done by the individual or collectively by the "state") violates every notion of human dignity. Would a reasonable person conclude that the practice is inhumane or barbaric? While the death penalty has been abandoned by most of the world, we apparently do not have a consensus in this country that capital punishment is cruel.

B. Is the Practice of Assisted Suicide Cruel?

While many consider assisted suicide to be an expression of compassion, the practice is quite controversial. Assisted suicide is suicide with the aid of another person, particularly a doctor. In *Washington v. Glucksberg*[145]the Supreme Court unanimously held that a right to assisted suicide was not protected by the Due Process Clause of the Fourteenth Amendment to the United States Constitution. Nevertheless, at least 10 states have "death with dignity" laws.[146] These laws are intended to give terminally ill patients dignity, control and peace of mind in their final days by allowing mentally competent, adult patients with a prognosis of less than six months to live to voluntarily request and receive medication to bring about their death.

Consider for a moment whether the practice can meet the definition of cruelty. Those individuals who subscribe to a culture of life, tend to be concerned with the subtle message being sent to the elderly and infirm in states which allow for assisted suicide. The worry is that elderly or infirm persons might view themselves as a burden on their families or society. That view, coupled with the right on the part of another individual to assist in the taking of life, creates a very problematic dynamic. Consent to the assisted suicide may very well be the product of duress,

---

[145] 521 U.S. 702 (1997).

[146] California, Colorado, District of Columbia, Hawaii, Maine, New Jersey, New Mexico, Oregon, Vermont and Washington.

coercion or undue influence, not to mention the product of the loss of self-worth and desire to avoid being seen as a financial or emotional drain on others.

Under those circumstances, it would seem cruel to exploit the elderly or infirm person by assisting them in a suicide and thereby intentionally inflicting death without a moral justification. On the other hand, in the context of an assisted suicide where the decedent was suffering from constant, uncontrollable pain, and the consent was freely given, that would not constitute cruelty because the taking of life would be morally justified. Statutes of this nature contain protections which are designed to ensure that the terminally ill patient remains in charge of end-of-life care decisions. Furthermore, this is not a widespread or common practice. For example, in California in 2020, out of over 39.5 million residents,[147] there were only 435 deaths from these prescriptions.[148]

While most states ban the practice, a majority of Americans find the practice acceptable. In a May 2016 Gallup poll, 69% of Americans said they agree that "when a person has a disease that cannot be cured...doctors should be allowed by law to end the patient's life by some painless means if the patient and their family request it."[149] In 2014, a Harris Poll found that 74 percent of Americans agree that the terminally ill have the right to choose to end their own life.[150] Accordingly, there certainly does not seem to be a consensus that assisted suicide is inhumane or barbaric.

---

[147] *QuickFacts California*, U.S. CENSUS BUREAU, https://www.census.gov/quickfacts/CA (last accessed Feb. 25, 2022).
[148] *State Report Navigator*, DEATH WITH DIGNITY, https://deathwithdignity.org/state-report-navigator/ (last accessed Feb. 25, 2022).
[149] Art Swift, *Euthanasia Still Acceptable to Solid Majority in U.S.*, GALLUP (June 24, 2016), https://news.gallup.com/poll/193082/euthanasia-acceptable-solid-majority.aspx.
[150] Dennis Thompson, *Most Americans Agree with Right-to-Die Movement*, STAGWELL (Dec. 5, 2014), https://theharrispoll.com/by-dennis-thompson-healthday-reporter/.

C. Is the Practice of Genital Mutilation Cruel?

According to the World Health Organization, the practice of female genital mutilation comprises all procedures that involve "partial or total removal of the external female genitalia, or other injury to the female genital organs for non-medical reasons."[151] The practice has no medical or health benefits for girls or women.[152]

The practice obviously harms girls and women in many ways. It involves removing and damaging healthy and normal female genital tissue, and interferes with the natural functions of girls' and women's bodies.[153] Immediate complications can include: severe pain, excessive bleeding, genital tissue swelling, fever, infections e.g., tetanus, urinary problems, wound healing problems, injury to surrounding genital tissue, shock and in some instances, death.[154] The long-term complications can include: urinary problems (painful urination, urinary tract infections), vaginal problems (discharge, itching, bacterial vaginosis and other infections), menstrual problems (painful menstruations, difficulty in passing menstrual blood, etc.), scar tissue and keloid, sexual problems (pain during intercourse, decreased satisfaction, etc.), increased risk of childbirth complications (difficult delivery, excessive bleeding, caesarean section, need to resuscitate the baby, etc.) and newborn deaths, need for later surgeries: for example, the sealing or narrowing of the vaginal opening may lead to the practice of cutting open the sealed vagina later to allow for sexual intercourse and childbirth (deinfibulation).[155] Sometimes genital tissue is stitched again several times, including after childbirth, hence the woman goes through repeated opening and

---

[151] *Female Genital Mutilation*, WORLD HEALTH ORG. (Jan. 21, 2022), https://www.who.int/news-room/fact-sheets/detail/female-genital-mutilation.
[152] *Id.*
[153] *Id.*
[154] *Id.*
[155] *Id.*

closing procedures, further increasing both immediate and long-term risks, and psychological problems (depression, anxiety, post-traumatic stress disorder, low self-esteem, etc.).[156]

While the practice is most common in Africa, Asia, and the Middle East, it is also widespread in immigrant communities and metropolitan areas in the United States, and was performed by doctors regularly until the 1980s.[157] Although performed for primarily socio-cultural and religious reasons, this practice is quite clearly cruel.[158] Not surprisingly, female genital mutilation is no longer consistent with law in the U.S. In 1996, 18 U.S.C. § 116 was passed making female genital mutilation an unlawful assault under federal criminal law. The statute was amended effective January 5, 2021, to make the prohibition even stronger.

What about removing a baby boy's foreskin from his penis? Is that cruel? Circumcision is the surgical removal of the skin covering the tip of the penis. According to the Mayo Clinic, the procedure is fairly common for newborn boys in certain parts of the world, including the United States. For some families, circumcision is a religious ritual. The procedure can also be a matter of family tradition, personal hygiene or preventive health care. For others, however, circumcision seems unnecessary and disfiguring. While there appear to be modest health care benefits associated with the procedure, it is becoming increasingly controversial. Whether it is cruel, like female genital mutilation (sometimes called female circumcision), is an interesting question. The law clearly allows it. Perhaps baby boys don't have as good a lobbyist, but the law certainly treats male genital mutilation differently. Unlike female genital mutilation, it is not a federal crime to painfully remove part of a baby boy's genitals for the sake of family or religious tradition.

---

156 *Id.*

157 *See* Howard Goldberg et al., *Female Genital Mutilation/Cutting in the United States: Updated Estimates of Women and Girls at Risk, 2012*, 131 PUB. HEALTH REPS. 340, 341 (2016).

158 *See id.*

D. Is Abortion Cruel?

The constitutional law of abortion in the United States fundamentally changed with the Supreme Court's 2022 decision in *Dobbs v. Jackson Women's Health Organization.*[159] In *Dobbs*, the Court held that the U.S. Constitution does not confer a fundamental right to abortion, expressly overruling *Roe v. Wade* and *Planned Parenthood v. Casey.*[160] The Court rejected the view that abortion is protected under the Fourteenth Amendment's Due Process Clause, concluding that such a right is neither explicitly enumerated in the Constitution nor "deeply rooted in this Nation's history and tradition."[161] As a result, abortion is no longer subject to heightened constitutional scrutiny under federal law.

In the wake of *Dobbs*, regulatory authority over abortion has largely reverted to the states, subject only to general constitutional constraints such as rational-basis review and other independent constitutional provisions (e.g., equal protection, vagueness, or procedural due process in specific applications). The pre-*Dobbs* frameworks of viability and "undue burden" are no longer controlling. States are now free to prohibit abortion entirely, regulate it extensively, or protect access as a matter of state law.

This shift has produced a highly fragmented legal landscape. Many states have enacted or enforced near-total abortion bans, often pursuant to "trigger laws" that became effective upon the overruling of *Roe*. Other states permit abortion only up to early gestational limits with limited exceptions. Conversely, a number of states have affirmatively protected abortion access through statutes or state constitutional amendments, often grounding those protections in explicit privacy

---

159 597 U.S. 215 (2022).
160 *Id.* at 227–28.
161 *Id.* at 231.

provisions, liberty clauses, or guarantees of bodily autonomy under state constitutions. State courts have thus become the primary fora for abortion-related constitutional litigation.

At the federal level, Congress has not enacted comprehensive abortion legislation establishing nationwide standards, and post-*Dobbs* constitutional challenges to abortion restrictions face substantial doctrinal obstacles. However, federal law remains relevant in ancillary ways, particularly through regulatory authority and preemption doctrines. For example, litigation concerning the FDA's approval and regulation of medication abortion—most notably *FDA v. Alliance for Hippocratic Medicine*[162]—has addressed issues of standing and administrative law rather than recognizing any substantive constitutional right to abortion. The Supreme Court's resolution of that case left federal approval of mifepristone intact but did not alter the core holding of *Dobbs*.

Another emerging area of dispute involves interstate conflicts, including state "shield laws" designed to protect providers who offer abortion services to out-of-state patients and efforts by restrictive states to extend enforcement beyond their borders. These disputes raise unresolved questions concerning extraterritorial regulation, federalism, and the Dormant Commerce Clause, though no definitive Supreme Court doctrine has yet emerged.

In sum, abortion is no longer constitutionally protected under federal law, and its legality now depends primarily on state constitutions, state statutes, and political processes. The result is a patchwork regime marked by sharp geographic disparities, ongoing litigation, and continued uncertainty. Unless Congress enacts federal legislation or the Supreme Court revisits its

[162] 602 U.S. ___, 144 S. Ct. 1540 (2024).

substantive due process jurisprudence, abortion law in the United States will remain decentralized, contested, and predominantly state-driven.

This essay does not tackle the question of whether abortion is or should be lawful or Constitutional. Neither does this essay address whether abortion is moral. Rather, the focus here is slightly different and on the question of whether and under what circumstances abortion is cruel.

We are killing babies on an industrial scale in this country. It would seem cruel to dismember a living (though unborn) human being and vacuum them out of the uterus. This practice is legal in many jurisdictions. Fittingly, however, the practice of partially birthing a baby and killing it by severing its spinal cord with scissors (partial birth abortion) has been prohibited since 2003 by federal law.[163]

Without regard to the countervailing interests at play (and they are considerable in weight and importance), and in the abstract only, does legal abortion sound like cruelty? It would seem to meet all elements of my definition of cruelty.[164]

It surely constitutes the intentional infliction of unimaginable physical pain and/or death on the baby, a vulnerable human being incapable of defending themself. The American Congress of Obstetricians and Gynecologists, representing more than 57,000 ob-gyns and partners in women's health, states that a fetus can feel pain at approximately 24 weeks of gestation.[165] Others have studied the question and opine that a fetus can feel pain as early at 12 weeks of gestation.[166] Therefore, it seems clear that late term abortions performed all the way up to birth involve

---

[163] The Partial-Birth Abortion Ban of 2003, 18 U.S.C. §1531, was held to be constitutional by the U.S. Supreme Court in *Gonzales v. Carhart*, 550 U.S. 124 (2007).
[164] *See supra* p. 12.
[165] *See Facts are Important: Fetal Pain*, THE AMERICAN COLL. OF OBSTETRICIANS AND GYNECOLOGISTS, https://www.acog.org/advocacy/facts-are-important/fetal-pain (last accessed Feb. 25 2022).
[166] Stuart WG Derbyshire & John C Bockmann, *Reconsidering Fetal Pain*, 46 J. MED. ETHICS, 3,4 (2020).

procedures which inflict pain on the baby.[167] There is good evidence that abortions performed before viability also inflict pain on the baby. On the other hand, abortions performed before 12 weeks cause death but without the experience of pain.

Moreover, the practice can inflict emotional pain on the father of the baby. Where an abortion is performed with the knowledge of, but without the consent of, the father of the baby, surely that act has the potential of having a significant negative impact on the emotional well-being of the father whose offspring is being killed. Finally, the aborting mother can also be the victim of extreme emotional distress at the time of the abortion or following, especially where the decision to seek an abortion was the product of lack of knowledge on the part of the mother or coercion, duress or undue influence exerted on the mother. Abortion laws do no contain the safeguards against this phenomenon that the death with dignity laws have.

While it lacks the element of pleasure being taken by the abortionist, abortion nevertheless seems clearly barbaric, inhumane and an outrage to many. Of course, to others it is merely healthcare.

Neither does the procedure seem "necessary" or in furtherance of a moral end, except where the pregnancy places the health or life of the mother at stake. According to the Guttmacher Institute, almost 862,300 babies were aborted in 2017 in this country.[168] At its zenith in 1990, a total of 1,429,000 babies were being aborted per year in the U.S.[169] In New York State nearly one out of every four pregnancies end in abortion, and 37 percent of resident abortions are performed

---

[167] According to an article by Stuart W G Derbyshire, for the US National Library of Medicine, National Health Institutes, neuroanatomical pathways necessary for processing pain, similar to those observed in adults and older children, could be in place by 23 weeks' gestation. *See Can Fetuses Feel Pain?* 332 BMJ 909, 910 (2006).
[168] *Induced Abortion in the United States*, GUTTMACHER INST., https://www.guttmacher.org/fact-sheet/induced-abortion-united-states (last accessed Feb. 26, 2022).
[169] John Elflein, *Number of legal abortions reported in the U.S. from 1973 to 2019*, STATISTA (Dec. 2, 2021), https://www.statista.com/statistics/185274/number-of-legal-abortions-in-the-us-since-2000/.

on Black women.[170] It is highly doubtful that many of these abortions were occasioned by the necessity of saving the mother's life or health. In states like Vermont, which has radical abortion laws, abortions are theoretically allowed up to the point of birth, based on the abortionist's judgment regarding viability.[171]

That's real cruelty, but generally consistent with law. Almost nothing is done to prevent this cruel practice in most states during the early phases of a pregnancy, while the law differs from state to state in the case of later term abortion.

The legality of this cruel practice is a function of the fact that there are countervailing interests. That is, the well-being or the desire of the mother are interests which must be measured and balanced against the cruelty to the baby and/or the father in abortion. The question becomes: The mother's health notwithstanding, would it be cruel to require the mother to forego abortion and instead to carry the baby to term and deliver it? What about in the context of rape or incest? Is the law attempting to balance the relative cruelties associated with the predicament of an unwanted pregnancy? In the balancing, the interests of the mother seem to be given significantly more weight than those of the baby and the father. Perhaps this difference is the result of the objectification of the baby as less than human – merely a "fetus" or clump of cells. Is such a differential in balancing warranted?

---

[170] Tessa Longbons, *Abortion Reporting: New York (2017)*, CHARLOTTE LOZIER INST. (Dec. 19, 2019), https://lozierinstitute.org/abortion-reporting-new-york-2017/.
[171] Katey Price, *Six States and Their Radical Approaches to Abortion Law*, CHARLOTTE LOZIER INST. (June 25, 2020), https://lozierinstitute.org/six-states-and-their-radical-approaches-to-abortion-law/#_edn4.

E. Is Homelessness Cruel?

As of 2017, there were an estimated 553,743 homeless people in the United States on any given night, according to the National Alliance to End Homelessness.[172] And the problem is increasing.[173] Many of our major cities are all but overrun by the homeless.[174] Overall, 66.7% of the total homeless population of the United States consists of single individuals, with the remaining 33.3% being families.[175] Many are veterans, who have served and sacrificed for this country.

The top four causes of homelessness are lack of affordable housing, unemployment, poverty and low wages.[176] With deinstitutionalization of the mentally ill and disabled in the 1980s, many of the chronic homeless people suffer from mental illness and/or addiction. Some homeless find themselves out on the street temporarily for economic reasons. Many are resistant to the notion of staying in a shelter, and some are prevented from doing so due to their condition.

They live in tents, cardboard boxes and under overpasses. They relieve themselves on the streets and sidewalks. Some beg, some steal and others offer themselves out as prostitutes. They have no privacy or security in their living arrangements, and they are subject to the elements. In any event, their living conditions are squalid and their lives are painful and full of suffering.

Other than federal housing assistance and other feeble attempts to solve the aesthetic problem from the perspective of the non-homeless, very little in the way of effective legal steps have been taken in our major metropolitan areas to alleviate this suffering. The law does not address the problem squarely, and it is certainly not a meaningful part of the solution. As with gun

---

[172] *The State of Homelessness in America*, NAT'L ALL. TO END HOMELESSNESS, https://endhomelessness.org/homelessness-in-america/homelessness-statistics/state-of-homelessness-report-legacy/ (last accessed Feb. 26, 2022).

[173] *See id.*

[174] Some prefer the term "unhoused" or other euphemistic terms rather than "homeless." As most of the pertinent literature uses the term "homeless," this Article will as well.

[175] *Homeless Population by State 2022*, WORLD POPULATION REV., https://worldpopulationreview.com/state-rankings/homeless-population-by-state (last accessed Feb. 26, 2022).

[176] *Id.*

violence in major urban areas like Chicago, the legal system has done very little to solve the problem.

There is no good reason for having failed for decades to solve the homelessness problem. Homelessness on the scale we are experiencing it today is certainly not necessary. A society as wealthy as this one can certainly afford to solve this problem by making more affordable housing available together with the provision of concomitant services. It is obviously inhumane and violative of human dignity not to.

It strikes me that this clearly constitutes cruelty. This constitutes the willful or intentional withholding of aid to avoid severe physical or mental pain and suffering; done without necessity or reasonable moral justification; with the end result being regarded by reasonable people as inhumane or violative of human dignity.

F. Is Firing an Employee for No Reason Cruel?

Not that it probably happens with any great frequency, but it is perfectly legal to discharge an employee for no reason whatsoever under the employment at-will doctrine, recognized in all but one state. The United States is peculiar in this regard among Western industrialized nations.

Most employees don't know that. There are many misconceptions regarding the at-will employment doctrine among employees. The vast majority of at-will employees wrongly believe that they have far more job protections than they do.[177] According to a study by Professor Pauline Kim, 89% of workers incorrectly believe they are protected from being fired for a boss "personally disliking" them; 82% believe hiring someone else for less is illegal; 79% believe being fired in

[177] Pauline T. Kim, *Bargaining with Imperfect Information: A Study of Worker Perceptions of Legal Protection in an At-Will World*, 83 CORNELL L. REV. 105, 110 (1997-98).

retaliation for reporting another employee's theft is illegal; and 87% believe being fired on belief of theft when employee could prove innocence is illegal.[178]

Since at least 1877, the doctrine has existed and been supported by the notion that it promotes freedom of contract and freedom in the employment market. It allows employers to terminate poor-performing employees without experiencing bureaucratic delays and unwarranted transaction costs. It has historically been seen to comport with the *laissez-faire* American belief that both employees and employers prefer to have an at-will relationship versus increased job security. From the field of law and economics, Richard Epstein defended the at-will employment doctrine as helping sort workers into their most-productive positions.[179] Epstein argued that the at-will rule allows employers to discharge unproductive workers without the expense required in a just-cause regime and this prevents inefficiencies caused by low-effort or low ability workers.[180] He argues that good workers are protected by the profit-maximizing incentives of employers to keep productive workers.[181] Likewise, Judge Richard Posner has praised the doctrine for its positive effect on the economy.[182] A number of other commentators have expressed positive aspects of the doctrine.[183]

But is it cruel? The obvious downside to the doctrine is the lack of employment security it provides to both parties, but particularly to the employee. Because of the significant differential in bargaining power between large employers and individual employees, employees are very often in a "take-it-or-leave-it" predicament in their employment regarding the terms and conditions of

---

[178] *See id.* at 134.
[179] *See* Richard A. Epstein, *In Defense of the Contract at Will*, 51 U. CHI. L. REV. 947, 969 (1984).
[180] *See id.* at 951-52.
[181] *See id.* at 973.
[182] RICHARD A. POSNER, OVERCOMING LAW, 305-11 (1995).
[183] *See, e.g.*, J.H. Verkerke, *Discharge, in* ENCYCLOPEDIA OF LAW AND ECONOMICS 448 (Kenneth G. Dau-Schmidt et al. eds., 2nd ed. 2009); ALAN HYDE, WORKING IN SILICON VALLEY xvi–xvii, 92–96 (Routledge 2015).

that employment.[184] The rule allows for arbitrary and capricious actions by employers depriving their employees of their livelihood.

There would seem to generally be a high risk of the infliction of great mental suffering on an employee discharged without cause and for no good reason, especially if that employee was unable to find a replacement job immediately – as most employees live paycheck to paycheck. By definition, there would be no necessity or moral justification for the act. If not done merely arbitrarily, it would have to be done maliciously or for some degenerate pleasure. Finally, such a deprivation is clearly an affront to human dignity. Accordingly, the act meets my definition of cruelty.

But the law allows it in all but one U.S. jurisdiction – Montana. The Montana Wrongful Discharge from Employment Act of 1987 (WDEA),[185] created a cause of action for employees who believe that they were terminated without good cause.[186] Shouldn't good cause be the standard for discharge throughout the country if cruelty of this nature is to be avoided?

G. Is Invidious Discrimination Cruel?

Among the societal ills we face, invidious discrimination in education, voting, employment, public accommodations and application of justice on the basis of race, gender, age, disability and a handful of other immutable characteristics is one of the most intractable and destructive. The question here is whether it is cruel and what the law is doing to prohibit it.

---

[184] Matthew T. Bodie, *Taking Employment Contracts Seriously*, 50 SETON HALL L. REV. 1261, 1266 (2020) (citing Aditi Bagchi, *The Myth of Equality in the Employment Relation*, 2009 MICH. ST. L. REV. 579, 580 (2009)).
[185] MONT. CODE. ANN. §§ 39–2–901 to 914 (2021).
[186] *See* Donald C. Robinson, *The First Decade of Judicial Interpretation of the Montana Wrongful Discharge from Employment Act (WDEA)*, 57 MONT. L. REV. 375, 376 (1996).

It is not a leap to posit that such discrimination is cruel. The practice clearly meets the elements of my definition. It is generally intentional, or at least adverse treatment (as compared with adverse impact) discrimination is intentional. It inflicts mental suffering in those affected. It is unnecessary. It has no moral justification. It is sometimes practiced for the purpose of degenerate pleasure. Few things are more clearly an infringement on human dignity than being treated as less than human by invidious discrimination.

Fittingly, the law is highly protective against most forms of invidious discrimination. The law in this regard takes the form of federal and state constitutional provisions, federal and state statutes, executive orders and the common law. Moreover, the federal and many state governments have created agencies, like the Equal Employment Opportunity Commission, whose mission is to stamp out these practices in the contexts of employment and public accommodations. Suffice it to say that society takes this problem seriously from a legal standpoint. Since the 1960s when the federal Civil Rights Act of 1964[187] was passed, discrimination in employment, education, programs, voting and public accommodation has been reduced considerably. The Americans with Disabilities Act of 1990[188] and the Rehabilitation Act of 1973[189] provided similar protection to those with disabilities.

Many would say that these forms of discrimination still exist at intolerable levels. For example, some point to the federal and state criminal justice systems and to the disparity in the way it treats Black suspects and defendants. There is a general consensus in our society that, due to either subconscious bias or malicious motives, Black suspects and defendants are treated less favorably by the criminal justice system than are Whites. Observers allege that Black suspects are

[187] 42 U.S.C. §§ 1981 to 2000h-6.
[188] 42 U.S.C. §§ 12101-12213.
[189] 29 U.S.C. §§ 701-706.

shot by police at a higher rate than are White suspects. They allege that Black drivers are pulled over more often by police than are White drivers as the result of racial profiling. They also allege that Blacks are more aggressively prosecuted and sentenced than White defendants in criminal cases. Were that true, it would constitute pure cruelty.

The media tends to be attracted to incidents of White officers shooting Black suspects, and there are any number of anecdotal stories of this form of bias. In fact, the Black Lives Matter movement/organization was formed largely in response to instances of Black suspects being shot to death by police officers.[190] The heinous murder of George Floyd by a White police officer in Minneapolis is a glaring example, as is the justified shooting of Michael Brown by a White police officer in Ferguson, Missouri.

It is also true that the population of inmates in federal and state prisons in this country appears skewed heavily toward Blacks.

At first glance, the situation would appear dire. The statistics bear some of this out and throw a wet blanket on other claims.

---

[190] Interestingly, some of the most high-profile instances were found to be justified. Take, for instance, the case of 18-year-old Black man, Michael Brown, who was shot to death by a White police officer in Ferguson, Missouri in 2014. The facts of the altercation were disputed by many witnesses, but the FBI investigation, and a state grand jury investigation, found no basis on which to indict the police officer. This case ignited unrest in Ferguson and across the country and garnered national interest. Likewise, the case of Breonna Taylor, a 26-year-old Black woman who was fatally shot in her Louisville, Kentucky apartment in 2020 by White police officers, led to protests across the country. A grand jury declined to indict the officers for Taylor's death. Former Louisville Metro Police officer Brett Hankison was convicted in November 2024 of violating Breonna Taylor's federal civil rights during the botched raid and was sentenced on July 21, 2025, to 33 months in federal prison, followed by three years of supervised release, for his role in the raid. Taylor was killed on March 13, 2020, when seven plainclothes Louisville Metro Police Department officers arrived at her apartment to serve a search warrant in a narcotics investigation centered on her ex-boyfriend. Whether or not officers announced themselves as law enforcement is disputed. Taylor's boyfriend, Kenneth Walker, believing an intruder was breaking in, fired a warning shot from a legally-owned handgun that hit Sgt. Jonathan Mattingly in the leg. Officers returned fire, fatally shooting Taylor. Hankison was one of three officers who fired bullets that night. Hankison did not shoot Taylor but fired 10 shots into a window and a sliding glass door that were covered in blinds. Three bullets went into an adjoining apartment where a pregnant woman lived with her partner and 5-year-old child. Hankison was previously found not guilty on state charges of wantonly endangering Taylor's neighbors in early 2022. His first federal trial ended in a mistrial in November 2023 after the jury failed to reach a verdict on any charges. In his second trial, he was found not guilty of violating the civil rights of Taylor's neighbors.

The Stanford Open Policing Project collected statistics and analyzed the rates at which police stop motorists in locations across the country, relative to the population in those areas. The data show that officers generally stop black drivers at higher rates than white drivers. This broad pattern persists even after controlling for the drivers' age and gender.[191]

Concerning arrest and incarceration rates, the Sentencing Project's Report to the United Nations states:

> African Americans are more likely than white Americans to be arrested; once arrested, they are more likely to be convicted; and once convicted, and they are more likely to experience lengthy prison sentences. African-American adults are 5.9 times as likely to be incarcerated than whites . . . . As of 2001, one of every three black boys born in that year could expect to go to prison in his lifetime, ... compared to one of every seventeen white boys. Racial and ethnic disparities among women are less substantial than among men but remain prevalent.[192]

The United States Justice Department investigated numerous municipal police departments throughout the country for racial discrimination in the application of criminal justice. In 2021, the United States Secretary of State invited the United Nations to conduct an investigation into structural racism in the U.S. criminal justice system.[193]

It would appear that the type of structural racism which is alleged to exist in the criminal justice system would be the type of discrimination which is most commonly affected by adverse impact, and not adverse treatment, based on race. Thus, it would meet the alternate definition of

---

191 *Findings*, STAN. OPEN POLICING PROJECT, https://openpolicing.stanford.edu/findings/ (last accessed Feb. 26, 2022); Emma Pierson et al., *A Large-scale Analysis of Racial Disparities in Police Stops Across the United States*, 4 NATURE HUM. BEHAV. 736, 737 (2020) (finding in a study of nearly 100 million traffic stops that after normalizing for age, gender, and other variables, black drivers were stopped more often than white drivers).
192 THE SENTENCING PROJECT, REPORT OF THE SENTENCING PROJECT TO THE UNITED NATIONS SPECIAL RAPPORTEUR ON CONTEMPORARY FORMS OF RACISM, RACIAL DISCRIMINATION, XENOPHOBIA, AND RELATED INTOLERANCE 1 (2018) (citing E. Ann Carson, *Prisoners in 2016*, BUREAU OF JUSTICE STATISTICS, 8 tbl.6 (2018)), https://www.sentencingproject.org/wp-content/uploads/2018/04/UN-Report-on-Racial-Disparities.pdf.
193 REUTERS, *U.S. State Department Invites U.N. Racism Investigators to Visit U.S.* (July 13, 2021, 9:57 PM), https://www.reuters.com/world/us/us-state-department-invites-un-racism-investigators-visit-us-2021-07-14/.

cruelty which includes the element of willful or intentional withholding of aid to prevent suffering. Stated in another way, the government has failed to take meaningful action to address the disparate impact.

On the other hand, most acts of employment discrimination, public accommodation discrimination and other forms of discrimination which are inflicted intentionally would constitute instance of cruelty on the basis of intentional infliction of mental suffering. In these cases, the government has taken efficacious steps to remediate the problem, but individual acts of cruelty still occur.

H. Is the Rampant Gun Violence in Chicago Cruel?

Year after year, the City of Chicago regularly experiences weekends in which numerous people are shot at random by hoodlums in gangland-style mayhem. Chicago leads its peer cities in these statistics. According to crime statistics maintained by the Chicago Police Department, at least 2764 people were shot in Chicago in 2020, and that number is higher for 2021, part way through the year.[194] That's real cruelty. While nominally illegal, the legal apparatus in Chicago and Cook County has for years done precious little to bring an end to this violent phenomenon. Marginalizing this dynamic as the acts of gang members toward each other seems to alleviate the desire to take meaningful legal action to quell it. This is an abject failure of proper law enforcement and justice administration coupled with a socio-economic environment that foments this type of cruelty. This is not necessary, and there is simply no moral justification for allowing this to continue.

---

[194] *CompStat*, CHI. POLICE DEP'T (2021), https://home.chicagopolice.org/wp-content/uploads/1_PDFsam_CompStat-Public-2021-Week-44.pdf.

I. Is the Deportation of Illegal Aliens Cruel?

The question of whether deportation of illegal aliens constitutes cruelty is uncomfortable, politically charged, and easily obscured by abstraction. Yet under the analytical framework developed in this Article—focusing on intentional infliction of severe suffering, lack of necessity or moral justification, and violations of human dignity—it is a question that must be confronted directly rather than evaded through slogans or euphemisms.

At the outset, deportation is not punishment in the traditional criminal-law sense. The Supreme Court has long characterized removal as a civil, regulatory consequence of unlawful presence rather than a penal sanction.[195] Nevertheless, deportation undeniably inflicts severe physical, psychological, and emotional suffering in many cases. Families are separated, livelihoods destroyed, individuals are returned to countries where they may face poverty, violence, or persecution, and children—often United States citizens—suffer trauma through forced separation from parents. These harms are not incidental; they are foreseeable, systemic, and in many cases devastating.

Applying the first element of cruelty, deportation plainly involves the intentional infliction of serious mental and emotional suffering. While the government does not typically act with sadistic pleasure, intent under this framework does not require malice or enjoyment. It is sufficient that the suffering is knowingly inflicted as a consequence of state action. Deportation is a deliberate act, carried out with full awareness of its likely human consequences.

[195] *See, e.g.*, *Fong Yue Ting v. United States*, 149 U.S. 698, 730 (1893) ("The order of deportation is not a punishment for crime."); *Harisiades v. Shaughnessy*, 342 U.S. 580, 594 (1952) ("Deportation, however severe its consequences, has been consistently classified as a civil rather than a criminal procedure."); *INS v. Lopez-Mendoza,* 468 U.S. 1032, 1038 (1984) (describing deportation as "a purely civil action"); *Padilla v. Kentucky*, 559 U.S. 356, 365 (2010) (reaffirming the civil nature of removal proceedings while acknowledging their severity).

The more difficult inquiry is whether deportation lacks necessity or reasonable moral justification. Unlike gratuitous violence, deportation is justified by the state as necessary to enforce immigration laws, preserve national sovereignty, deter future unlawful entry, and maintain the integrity of the legal system. These are legitimate governmental interests. A sovereign nation has the right to control its borders, define the conditions of entry, and remove those who violate its laws. In the abstract, deportation therefore does not constitute cruelty per se, just as incarceration or taxation does not.

However, cruelty often emerges not from the existence of a lawful power, but from its manner, scope, and indifference to proportionality and human dignity. Deportation becomes cruel where it is imposed without meaningful consideration of necessity, proportionality, or individualized circumstances—particularly where the person has long-standing ties to the United States, has committed no violent crime, poses no threat to public safety, and where removal predictably results in extreme hardship to innocent third parties.

The violation of human dignity—the fourth element of cruelty—is where deportation most acutely implicates this framework. Treating individuals solely as legal abstractions ("illegal aliens") rather than as human beings with families, histories, and moral worth mirrors the very process of dehumanization that has historically enabled cruelty. Structural cruelty does not require conscious malice; it arises when bureaucratic systems prioritize efficiency and deterrence over humanity. Mass deportation policies, categorical exclusions, and rigid enforcement mechanisms risk crossing this line by transforming removal into an instrument of collective suffering rather than a narrowly tailored regulatory tool.

That said, deportation is not categorically cruel in the way torture or slavery is. Where removal is necessary to protect public safety, where due process is afforded, where humanitarian considerations are weighed, and where the suffering inflicted is proportionate to the legitimate governmental objective, deportation falls outside the definition of cruelty articulated in this Article. Conversely, deportation approaches cruelty where it is employed indiscriminately, without mercy, without proportionality, and without regard to foreseeable human devastation.

In the final analysis, deportation occupies the same uneasy space as other legally sanctioned harms examined in this Article. It is lawful. It is sometimes justified. Yet it carries an ever-present risk of cruelty when law substitutes abstraction for judgment and deterrence for dignity. The question is therefore not whether deportation can be cruel, but whether our legal system is sufficiently attentive to human dignity to ensure that, in practice, it is not.

XVIII. CONCLUSION

The law tends to be aimed at rooting out cruelty in most of its forms from our society. However, as we can see, cruelty is not always effectively prohibited by the law. There is no "zero tolerance policy" for cruelty. Sometimes, when the cruelty seems justified or warranted by countervailing interests, the law allows for it. Keep in mind, of course, that the very definition of cruelty requires that there be no necessity or furtherance of a moral end. Accordingly, the cruelty which I discuss – that which is legal due to countervailing interests or lack of societal will – is not necessary or in furtherance of a moral end. In most other instances, where there are no weighty opposing interests, cruelty is illegal.

All too often, however, as in the case of capital punishment and abortion, cruelty is not always prohibited by the law. In other instances (i.e., homelessness, racial discrimination and pervasive gang violence), the cruelty has no real countervailing interests and there is simply a lack of will or creativity necessary to solve the problem. The law effectively acquiesces in or allows those conditions to persist.

Since 1750 B.C., and Hammurabi's Code, the law has been attempting to protect human dignity but in a fashion which has not universally forbidden the application of cruelty. Surely the Roman practice of crucifixion would not withstand Eighth Amendment scrutiny as punishment. Neither would an eye for an eye pass general muster under modern U.S. law, except perhaps in the case of a life for a life in the context of capital punishment. But the principles of deterrence and retributive justice seem to justify the government killing a convicted criminal in cold blood and thereby warrants the ostensible cruelty in that instance. Additionally, capital punishment is, in the abstract, "usual" even though arguably cruel and therefore not generally violative of the Eighth Amendment.

In sum, through the law we have not come a long way in terms of rooting out cruelty from society. We have work to do in eliminating cruelty in the form of intentional invidious discrimination and willful failure to take action to rid our society of racial discrimination in the criminal justice system. We have virtually unrestrained gun violence in our major urban areas. We have record homelessness in our big cities with over half a million people experiencing homelessness on any given night. Moreover, we still have well over half a million abortions in this country year after year. That is against the general background of rapes, murders, robberies, kidnappings and other horribly cruel torts and crimes being perpetrated on a daily basis.

Cruelty is very much alive and well in twenty-first century America, and the law seems to be either agnostic to it or disposed in favor of it in far too many instances. On the other hand, significant progress in the form of legislation and enforcement has been made in other areas of the law (i.e., employment discrimination). Additionally, we no longer subject prisoners to egregious overcrowding conditions, and we no longer execute certain categories of convicted criminals, based upon their young age, mental capacity and the crime they committed.

Criminal and tort law remain what seems to be a relative constant, chipping away at cruelty for the most part one case at a time. But our culture seems to be headed in the wrong direction. Our culture has coarsened. Not surprisingly, our art has become much more caustic. We now see crucifixes submerged in urine, passing as critically acclaimed art.[196] We hear music that denigrates and celebrates violence against women. We see movies that portray stylized violence and graphic cruelty as mainstream entertainment. Our literature is no different. By any reasonable measure, it is very difficult to conclude that there has been much meaningful evolution on this subject as our society is said to mature.

In some ways, professional football is an apt metaphor for our modern society as it relates to cruelty and the rules that govern it. Just as the rules in the National Football League have been adjusted to protect the quarterbacks and other skilled players from unnecessary violence (and the resulting injuries), our legal system has adopted protections against certain instances of cruelty. We protect certain people and not others. However, the underlying exercise in football is admittedly fairly brutal, as it is with modern society.

Rules against taunting in the NFL penalize players for use of baiting or taunting acts or words that engender ill will between teams. Off the field fines, together with on-field penalties, combine to significantly punish teams and players for taunting and unsportsmanlike conduct – which would seem to be relatively minor infractions. On the other hand, the NFL crowds roar with excitement at the application of a brutal block or tackle, which generally are not a violation

---

[196] "Piss Christ" by Andres Serrano.

of the rules, unless leveled against a quarterback or defenseless receiver or consisting of "unnecessary roughness".

I am a fan of professional football, but for me it is a guilty pleasure. While I enjoy the finesse and skill of the players, I have to admit that I am also entertained by the hard-hitting action of the game. I appreciate the incongruence of my dispositions. Sometimes it seems that we get the small things right and fail to address the big things in football, but that's what makes it football. We seem to have that sort of legal relationship with cruelty in our modern society as well. We still hear echoes from the Roman Colosseum.

Published by Sterling Letter Press

ABOUT THE AUTHOR

Daniel S. Alcorn is a management-side labor and employment law attorney licensed in Texas, Arizona and Illinois. He currently practices Of Counsel with Davis & Campbell L.L.C. in Peoria, Illinois, where he maintains a subfocus in Artificial Intelligence law and policy. Dan previously practiced with Littler

Mendelson P.C., the world's largest management-side labor and employment law firm, after serving as Associate General Counsel – Employment Law for TORC Robotics, Inc. in Austin, Texas and in-house employment law counsel for State Farm Mutual Automobile Insurance Company in Bloomington, Illinois.

Dan has authored numerous legal articles published in law reviews, bar journals and other legal publications. Additionally, Dan has published several fiction and nonfiction works and novels.

Dan earned his B.A. in economics and philosophy from Knox College and his J.D. from Drake University Law School, where he served as Articles Editor of the Drake Law Review. More recently, Dan earned his graduate certificate from M.I.T. in Artificial Intelligence and its implications for business strategy. He is the founder and publisher of Sterling Letter Press, which champions writers who create works, fiction and nonfiction, which sit at the intersection of law, ethics, and the messier truths of human character, with the discipline of an argument and the pulse of a story.

Dan is married to Marcy Alcorn, and between them they have five wonderful children and one granddaughter with another grandchild on the way.

NOTES

www.ingramcontent.com/pod-product-compliance
Lightning Source LLC
LaVergne TN
LVHW060548061126
851857LV00017B/1946
9798997871123